CONDITIONS

AND

PLANNING

OBLIGATIONS

CONDITIONS

AND

PLANNING

OBLIGATIONS

by

Richard Langham
BA (Oxon)

Barrister

CLT PROFESSIONAL PUBLISHING
A DIVISION OF CENTRAL LAW TRAINING LTD

© **Richard Langham 1996**

Published by
CLT Professional Publishing
A Division of Central Law Training Ltd
Wrens Court
52-54 Victoria Road
Sutton Coldfield
Birmingham
B72 1SX

ISBN 1 85811 063 7

Typeset by Cheryl Zimmerman
Printed in Great Britain

Contents

Foreword

The origin of town and country planning control, as we now know it, lies in the Town and Country Planning Act 1947. The Second World War generated an ambition for massive social change and the 1947 Act was a product of this ambition. In effect it nationalised the common law right of a landowner to use and develop his land and subjected it to a system of control exercised through development plans and the need for planning permission. It was, and remains, a system of land use control.

Some aspects of this Act, now consolidated in 1990 legislation, have long since been repealed. Some subsequent alterations have come and gone. Ideas about the nature, content and extent of development plans have changed, very often. But the central theme of land use and development control has endured and grown. Recent years have witnessed a growing appreciation of our environment. Concern is widely expressed to preserve our buildings of merit, the countryside and wildlife, and most people believe passionately in the need to preserve and enhance the quality of life, both of this generation and for those to come. Much of the control needed to give effect to these sentiments is exercised through town and country planning legislation.

Perhaps not surprisingly, though arguably not necessarily, the volume of primary and subordinate legislation has grown to a daunting size and complexity, and is constantly changing. References to the High Court are common. Because the statutory system of control leaves much to the discretion of the decision-maker, whether the Secretary of State or the local planning authority, there is a mountain of documentation which contains the policies that the various decision-makers will apply in exercising that discretion. At Central Government level policies are mainly stated in Circulars and Planning Policy Guidance notes, and are applied to particular facts in numerous decisions on appeal to the Secretary of State. At local government level policies lie in the development plan created by each local planning authority, and these are often detailed and large.

Any professional who steps into this field of legislation needs, at least, to have a clear idea of the main strands of law and policy, and where he may find more necessary detail. The purpose of this series, written by specialists in the field, is to provide a basic, accessible and practical guide on a number of substantial topics in this field. This book is part of this series. I believe that a general practitioner, and some property owners, will find it helpful.

Lionel Read QC
1 Serjeants' Inn
November 1995

Preface

Much of the most interesting and difficult planning law concerns conditions and planning obligations. Topics like the purported implementation of planning permissions by works in breach of condition, the scope of *Grampian* conditions and the approach to be taken to planning gain have all exercised the appellate courts in recent years. The high level of judicial attention given to conditions and planning obligations reflects their immense practical importance. Together they constitute the ways in which qualifications and collateral obligations can be added to a grant of planning permission. Although quite different, they therefore naturally fall to be considered in one work.

This work aims to give a simple account of the law of conditions and planning obligations for the general practitioner. It eschews academic speculation, and seeks, where possible, to give a certain statement of the legal position. Where the case-law does not produce certainty, it endeavours to point this out.

Many topics involve detailed analysis of provisions of the 1990 Act. There is no substitute for the *ipsissima verba* of the Act, and, wherever possible, any discussion starts with the relevant statutory provisions. Important statutory words and provisions are highlighted in quotation marks.

The work is primarily concerned with the law rather than with the requirements of planning policy. Inevitably, it deals with general government policy in Circulars 11/95 and 16/91. Beyond this it does not attempt to give guidance on what conditions or planning obligations will be appropriate in planning terms in any particular case. Nor does the work deal with detailed questions of drafting. Drafting of planning obligations, in particular, is a highly intricate and specialised matter and not an appropriate subject for a work of this kind.

It is inevitably difficult to define the boundaries of a work on conditions and planning obligations. I have included a full discussion of implementation of planning permissions as background to a consideration of *Whitley (FG) & Sons Ltd* v *Secretary of State for Wales*. The area of enforcement is particularly difficult. Breach of Condition Notices plainly call for specific attention. However, enforcement of planning control is a vast topic, covering many subjects far removed from conditions or planning obligations. The work therefore gives only a general account of Enforcement Notices and Stop Notices. It identifies the circumstances in which criminal liability arises for breach of such notices, but does not cover such liability in any detail. It does not deal with Planning Contravention Notices, other requisitions for information, direct action by local planning authorities, criminal liability under sections 178 and 181 of the 1990 Act, or injunctions.

In addition, court procedure, the special provisions for mineral development, Crown lands and special planning zones and the particular problems of planning obligations created before 25 October 1991 are not covered.

The law is stated as at 22 August 1995.

Richard Langham
1 Serjeants' Inn,
London
August 1995

Table of Cases

CHAPTER I

Introduction

CHAPTER 1

Introduction

This chapter gives a broad overview of planning law relevant to conditions and planning obligations, and introduces important concepts and terms referred to in later chapters.

Planning law is entirely a creature of statute. The starting point is the **Town and Country Planning Act 1990** (as amended) which consolidates and amends earlier legislation.

The basic regime for planning control established by the Act is as follows.

Planning permission and development

1. Development

Subject to exceptions provided for by the Act, the carrying out of **development** on land requires a grant of **planning permission** (s 57(1)). "Development" covers two matters: the carrying out of building, engineering, mining or other **operations** on land; and the carrying out of a **material change of use** in buildings or on land (s 55(1)). Detailed provisions covering precise matters falling within and outwith these terms are contained in section 55. Activity which does not fall within the definition of "development" does not require the grant of planning permission.

2. The Use Classes Order and the General Permitted Development Order

There are two important exceptions to the requirement to obtain a grant of planning permission. The first arises as a result of section 55(2)(f), which provides that the Secretary of State can specify that certain changes of use do not involve development. Under this power the Secretary of State has made the **Use Classes Order 1987**. This contains 12 use classes, each comprised of a number of different uses of land and buildings. As a result of section 55(2)(f), change from one use to another use within the same use class does not constitute development, even though it may involve a material change of use of the land.

The second exception arises as a result of section 59 of the Act. This provides that the Secretary of State can make orders (known as "development orders") which grant planning permission for specified classes of development. Under this power he has made the **Town and Country Planning (General Permitted Development) Order 1995**, which grants planning permission for 33 identified types of development. Most of the types of development involve carrying out of operations, and cover matters like putting up fences, certain works within the curtilage of dwelling houses, small extensions to industrial buildings and works carried out by statutory undertakers. Some changes of use are also covered. The Order is intended to make it unnecessary to obtain an express grant of planning permission for trivial development. Unlike the Use Classes Order, the matters covered by this Order do constitute development within the meaning of section 55: that is why it is necessary for the Order to grant planning permission for them. Development covered by the Order is known as "permitted development". The Secretary of State can, by direction, withdraw permitted development rights with regard to specified areas. The consequence of the making of such a direction is that, within the area identified, specified categories of development that would ordinarily have planning permission as a result of the Order require an express grant of planning permission.

3. Full and outline planning permission

Often it is not sensible for a developer to prepare a fully designed scheme for proposed development before he knows whether planning permission will be granted for it. A procedure therefore exists for testing the acceptability of the principle of development, without involving consideration of all the details of a scheme. This is done by seeking **outline planning permission**[1]. This can only be granted for development consisting of the erection of a building. Such a permission will reserve for later approval by the local planning authority questions of siting, design, external appearance, means of access and/or landscaping. In this way the local planning authority can ensure that it retains control of these matters while granting a permission that accepts the principle of the relevant kind of development. The questions of siting, design, external appearance, means of access and/or landscaping reserved for later approval are known as **reserved matters**. If a planning permission is not an outline planning permission it is known as "full" planning permission.

4. Procedure for obtaining planning permission

Assuming that planning permission is required for contemplated development, an application for this must be made to the **local planning**

[1]See Arts 1, 3 and 4 of the Town and Country Planning (General Development Procedure) Order 1995.

authority. In areas with unitary local authorities, the local planning authority is the unitary authority. In other areas the local planning authority is usually the district or borough council. County councils are local planning authorities for certain specified types of development, most notably development involving mining operations.

Applications must be made on a standard form and give certain information[2]. The plans accompanying the application will form part of the application, as may the contents of accompanying correspondence.

If planning permission is refused by the local planning authority, or if the authority fails to deal with the application within a specified time, the developer can appeal to the **Secretary of State for the Environment**[3]. The appeal will, in most cases, be determined by an Inspector acting on behalf of the Secretary of State, and may involve the holding of a public inquiry. If the appeal is successful the inspector or the Secretary of State will grant planning permission for the development.

It is possible to seek planning permission for development that has already been carried out[4].

Conditions

1. Imposition of conditions
In theory a grant of planning permission need do no more than indicate that permission is granted for a particular development to be carried out on a particular site. In practice the local planning authority or the Secretary of State will impose **conditions** on the permission. Indeed, only a planning permission granted for development that has already been carried out can contain no conditions at all. Where the development has not already been carried out the Act itself stipulates that conditions should be imposed placing a time limit on the implementation of the permission[5]. Most grants of planning permission will contain other conditions.

Conditions are the principal means by which a planning authority can impose limits and controls on the development it is permitting. Where a development (unless controlled or regulated in some way) has the potential to cause disturbance or other types of harm, the imposition of conditions will probably be the means by which the authority ensures that such harm is not caused. A development may only be acceptable,

[2] See s 62; the Town and Country Planning (Applications) Regulations 1988; and the Town and Country Planning (General Development Procedure) Order 1995.
[3] s 78.
[4] s 73A.
[5] ss 91 and 92.

and so deserving of planning permission, if it is regulated and controlled in this way.

Conditions can be used to amend the scheme for which planning permission is sought by cutting down the scope of the development permitted by the permission.

2. Common types of condition
There are a number of common types of condition, some of which create particular legal problems. Common types of condition include the following:

Time limit on implementation
All planning permissions (except those for development already carried out) must have a condition imposing a time limit on implementation of the permission. In full planning permissions the condition will typically state:

> "The development hereby permitted shall be begun before the expiration of five years from the date of this permission."[6]

Conditions of this kind are particularly important. If such a condition is not complied with the planning permission lapses. It is therefore important to developers to know what works/activities will implement a planning permission. Difficult problems arise when a developer attempts to implement a planning permission by carrying out works that breach other conditions in the permission.

Condition requiring approval of reserved matters
Outline planning permissions will require the approval of reserved matters by means of a condition, for example:

> "Approval of details of design and external appearance of the building (hereinafter called the 'reserved matters') shall be obtained from the local planning authority."[7]

The approval of reserved matters does not count as a further grant of planning permission, but such approval can be made the subject of conditions.

Condition requiring approval of other matters
Reserved matters are not the only matters that can be left for subsequent approval by the local planning authority. A full or outline planning permission can require other matters not dealt with in the application to be approved by the local planning authority. A typical condition of this kind would be:

[6]Model condition 1 in Circular 11/95.   [7]Based on model condition 2 in Circular 11/95.

"Construction work shall not begin until a scheme for protecting the proposed dwellings from noise from the ... has been submitted to and approved by the local planning authority; all works which form part of the scheme shall be completed before any of the dwellings is occupied."[8]

Grampian condition

Sometimes development is not acceptable unless works which the developer cannot secure are carried out (*e.g.* infrastructure works on land beyond the developer's control). A condition cannot positively require the developer to do such works. However, the local planning authority can prevent any development from starting or being brought into use unless and until such works are carried out by imposing what is known as a *"Grampian"* condition[9]. Typically a *Grampian* condition designed to secure the carrying out of drainage works might state:

"Development shall not be begun until drainage works have been carried out in accordance with details to be submitted to and approved in writing by the local planning authority."[10]

Occupancy condition/personal planning permission

In appropriate circumstances a condition may restrict the person who may occupy a particular building. Typically an occupancy condition might limit occupation to an agricultural worker (in the case of a dwelling) or a local firm (in the case of commercial premises). A planning permission for a material change of use might be limited to use by a particular individual by condition.

Conditions can remove rights conferred by the General Permitted Development Order and the Use Classes Order.

Any condition in a planning permission must be imposed by express words. It is not possible to have implied conditions. Where planning permission is granted for the erection of a building, the planning permission can specify the purpose for which the building is to be used. If no such purpose is specified, the permission is construed as including permission to use the building for the purpose for which it is designed.[11]

3. Discharge/modification of conditions

If a developer is granted a planning permission which contains a condition that he is unable or unwilling to comply with he can appeal against the grant of planning permission to the Secretary of State. On

[8]Based on model condition 7 in Circular 11/95.
[9]After the decision in *Grampian Regional Council* v *City of Aberdeen* [1984] JPL 590.
[10]Model condition 40 in Circular 11/95.
[11]s 75(2) and (3).

such an appeal the Secretary of State considers afresh what permission, if any, should be granted to the developer. If the developer does not wish to put the whole permission at risk in this way, he must make a new application to the local planning authority to seek permission to carry out the development without complying with the offending condition[12]. On such an application the local planning authority can only consider what conditions should be imposed on the planning permission, and can remove or modify any of the conditions. If the local planning authority refuses his application, or fails to determine it in the specified time, the developer can appeal to the Secretary of State.

Enforcement of planning control

Carrying out development without the necessary planning permission, or failing to comply with a condition in a grant of planning permission, constitutes a **breach of planning control**[13]. A breach of planning control does not constitute a crime, but it can be restrained by injunction in the civil courts. In addition the local planning authority can serve an **enforcement notice** against any breach of planning control and/or a **breach of condition notice** against a breach of planning control arising from a breach of condition. Serving either kind of notice constitutes **taking enforcement action**[14]. Both notices take the form of an instruction to remedy the breach of planning control within a prescribed period. There are a number of significant differences between the two, the most important being that the recipient of an enforcement notice can appeal against it to the Secretary of State. No such right of appeal exists against a breach of condition notice. An enforcement notice is suspended while any appeal to the Secretary of State is determined. If the local planning authority wishes to ban certain activities, including some breaches of condition, from taking place before the period for compliance in an enforcement notice has expired, it can serve a **stop notice**. This is an instruction to cease the relevant activity almost immediately. Failure to comply with the requirements of an enforcement notice, a stop notice or a breach of condition notice constitutes a criminal offence.

If a breach of planning control continues for a certain specified period of time it becomes immune from enforcement action[15] and counts as **lawful** development[16].

[12] s 73.
[13] s 171A.
[14] s 171A.
[15] s 171B.
[16] s 191(2).

Planning obligations

There are certain limits on what can be achieved by imposing conditions. In particular, it is not possible to require a developer to make payments of money by condition. A requirement to pay money may need to be imposed before major development can be regarded as acceptable. For example, proposed development might be likely to overload existing infrastructure. The problem might be capable of being relieved by carrying out improvements works. The developer might be unable to carry out the works himself (either because he does not control the necessary land or because statutory powers will be needed), but might be willing to pay for the works to be done. A condition could not require that this funding should be provided.

The need for developers to be able to give binding undertakings covering matters that cannot be dealt with by conditions has long been recognised. For many years there was provision in the Planning Acts allowing local planning authorities and developers to enter into agreements related to the development or use of land. Such agreements bound the land owned by the developer, and were enforceable by the local planning authority. In 1991 the law in this area was modified significantly by the insertion of a new **section 106** into the 1990 Act. Under the new regime a developer can enter into legal obligations, binding on his land and covering matters that cannot be achieved by condition, either by agreement with the local planning authority *or unilaterally*. These obligations (whether created unilaterally or by agreement) are known as **planning obligations**. Certain formal requirements have to be satisfied to create a planning obligation.

Because of the wide range of matters that can be covered by planning obligations, and the suspicion that the offer of planning obligations can be used to "buy" grants of planning permission, the scope and use of planning obligations (and agreements under the predecessor provisions) have caused major controversy and litigation in recent years. This has culminated in the recent House of Lords' decision in *Tesco Stores Ltd* v *Secretary of State for the Environment and West Oxfordshire DC and Tarmac Provincial Properties Ltd* [1995] JPL 581 (see Chap 12).

A planning obligation is best understood as being similar to a covenant binding the land of the person entering into the obligation and enforceable by the local planning authority. Although a planning obligation usually accompanies a grant of planning permission, it does not have to. A planning obligation is quite separate from any planning permission that it accompanies. A landowner's failure to comply with a planning obligation binding his land does not constitute a breach of planning control. The failure to comply is a civil wrong and can be enforced by the local planning authority by injunction. The local planning authority also has certain rights to take direct action against the land itself.

The 1990 Act makes provision for landowners to seek the discharge or modification of planning obligation after a period of five years has elapsed[17].

Planning policy

Local planning authorities and the Secretary of State have policies which provide guidance on how the power to grant planning permission will be exercised. Councils formulate their policies by means of plans related to their areas, which have to be prepared following procedures laid down in the 1990 Act. These procedures are designed to ensure a high degree of public consultation. When all the procedures have been completed the plan can be adopted and forms part of the **development plan**. The plans prepared by district and borough councils, county councils and unitary authorities are known as **local plans**, **structure plans** and **unitary development plans** respectively. Such plans often have very little to say about the imposition of conditions or requirements for planning obligations. However, they may state that in certain circumstances certain types of condition will be imposed (*e.g.* to secure local needs housing). Also, a number of celebrated recent court cases have concerned planning obligations entered into as a result of development plan policies requiring that, in certain circumstances, developers would be expected to contribute to infrastructure costs.

The Secretary of State gives policy guidance by means of **circulars** and **planning policy guidance notes** (PPGs). Circulars tend to explain how particular planning powers should be operated (*e.g.* procedural regulations, or the rules on immunity from enforcement action) while PPGs tend to deal with particular planning issues (*e.g.* noise) or types of development (*e.g.* housing). **Circular 11/95** gives detailed guidance on the imposition of conditions. **Circular 16/91** gives detailed guidance on what may be offered or sought by means of planning obligation. Individual PPGs occasionally give guidance on conditions that can be imposed in particular situations.

Legal requirements

Statements of policy do not have the force of law. There may always be exceptional cases where policy does not have to be followed. If a

[17]ss 106A and B.

condition is imposed in breach of policy, this of itself means no more than that it may be inappropriate in planning terms.

Quite separate from the requirements of policy are the requirements of the law. These derive from the general principles of public law, which lay down how public authorities should exercise their powers, and from limits imposed by the 1990 Act. The law polices both what decisions a public authority is entitled to take, and the procedures by which it reaches those decisions. If a public authority's decision is unlawful a court may be prepared to quash it. The court has no power to substitute its own permission or condition. The effect of a successful court challenge is therefore that the original decision has no effect, and the relevant public authority has to reach a new decision.

When a developer is faced with an act of a local planning authority which he wishes to challenge on legal grounds, he must normally exhaust any right of appeal to the Secretary of State before starting court proceedings. On the appeal the Secretary of State must consider the legality of the local planning authority's action. The 1990 Act makes specific provision for bringing court challenges to decisions of the Secretary of State taken on such appeals[18]. The vast majority of cases in this area of the law are challenges of this type.

[18]ss 288 and 289.

PART I
Conditions

CHAPTER 2

Conditions and the Tests of Validity

CHAPTER 2

Conditions and the Tests of Validity

Introduction

The law lays down certain requirements that conditions have to meet. Non–compliance renders the condition unlawful and therefore invalid. Unless an invalid condition can be severed from the planning permission, the whole permission is invalid.

In addition, Government policy, in the form of Circular 11/95, lays down general guidance on the formulation of conditions, as well as of certain types of condition. Six tests, applicable to all conditions, are set out (these are discussed in detail in Chap 10). Some of these requirements cover the same subjects as the legal requirements discussed below. However, mere failure to comply with the Circular will not render a condition illegal[1].

Some of the legal restrictions on conditions can effectively be circumvented by using an appropriate *Grampian* condition.

Statutory provisions

The power to impose conditions comes from section 70(1) of the 1990 Act. This empowers local planning authorities, when dealing with applications for planning permission, to grant permission **subject to such conditions as they think fit**. This power is amplified by section 72(1) which states:

> **Without prejudice to the generality of Section 70(1), conditions may be imposed on the grant of planning permission under that Section—**
>
> (a) **for regulating the development or use of any land under the control of the applicant (whether or not it is land in respect of which the application was made) or requiring the carrying out of works on any such land, so far as appears to the local planning authority to be expedient for the purposes of or in connection with the development authorised by the permission;**

[1]*Ashford BC* v *Secretary of State for the Environment and Hume* [1992] JPL 363.

(b) for requiring the removal of any building or works authorised by the permission, or the discontinuance of any use of land so authorised, at the end of a specified period, and the carrying out of any works required for the reinstatement of the land at the end of that period.

In addition sections 91 and 92 require the imposition of conditions dealing with time limits on the implementation of full and outline planning permissions (these provisions are dealt with in Chap 4).

Grampian conditions

Grampian conditions are a kind of negative condition. They have assumed particular importance over the last decade because they extend the type of control that can be achieved by the imposition of conditions. A negative condition is one which prohibits the developer from doing something (as distinct from a positive condition which imposes an obligation on the developer to do something—*e.g.* to lay out a certain part of the site as car parking). Negative conditions can impose contingent prohibitions—typically that the development should not be begun or occupied until a certain event has occurred. Conditions of this type are called Grampian conditions following the House of Lords' decision in *Grampian Regional Council* v *City of Aberdeen* [1984] JPL 590. Often the event, if and when it occurs, will take place on different land. A condition may thus require that housing development on site A shall not be begun until an access to the proposed development over site B has been provided. The development depends on the occurring of the event, although the developer is under no obligation to secure the happening of the event.

Grampian conditions are of particular value when off-site infrastructure works have to be carried out before any development can be allowed to take place. It may well not be in the developer's power to carry out such works. The local planning authority cannot impose a positive obligation on the developer to do such works, but it can impose a *Grampian* condition preventing the development from starting until the necessary works have taken place. Such a *Grampian* condition is enforceable against the developer. If he attempts to start his development without the necessary works having been carried out, he will be in breach of planning control.

The result may be that a developer achieves the grant of a planning permission which he finds very difficult to implement. Until the House of Lords' decision in *British Railways Board* v *Secretary of State for the Environment and Hounslow LBC* [1993] JPL 342 it was thought that there had to be a "reasonable prospect'"of the relevant event(s) occurring before a *Grampian* condition could be validly imposed[2]. Indeed, such a test is mentioned in paragraph 40 of the Annex to Circular 11/95 and in paragraph 3 of Annex C of PPG 13. However, in that case it was decided that a *Grampian* condition would not automatically be unreasonable, and therefore invalid, merely because there was no reasonable prospect of it being complied with. The fact that a particular planning permission might be very difficult to implement does not mean that it should not be granted[3].

The *Newbury* tests

The wide terms of the statutory power to impose conditions has been explained and, to some extent, narrowed by judicial interpretation in case-law. In particular three tests of validity for conditions were laid down by the House of Lords in *Newbury DC* v *Secretary of State for the Environment* [1981] AC 578, based on the wording of the Act and previous authorities. These are that a condition must be imposed for a planning purpose, must fairly and reasonably relate to the development permitted, and must be reasonable[4]. These tests are considered below.

1. Imposed for a planning purpose

Section 72(1)(a) requires that conditions should be imposed for **regulating the use or development of land**. Conditions imposed under section 72(1)(b) will obviously relate directly to buildings or uses permitted by the relevant permission. A "planning purpose" will cover anything connected with the "use or development of land". Thus the statutory provisions themselves effectively require that conditions should be imposed for planning purposes.

"Planning purposes" will plainly embrace a very wide range of objectives. The aim of this test is to prevent conditions from being used to achieve purposes unrelated to the use, etc of land, or for ulterior purposes[5].

---

[2] *Daws v Secretary of State for the Environment* [1989] JPL 358; *Jones v Secretary of State for Wales* [1990] JPL 907; *Eagle Star v Secretary of State for the Environment* [1992] JPL 434; Court of Appeal in *British Railways Board* [1993] JPL 342.
[3] That is not to say that the difficulty of implementation would never be a relevant consideration for a local planning authority. The House of Lords contemplated that the prospect of implementation might be material if, for example, a local planning authority were faced with rival applications for desirable development, one of which would face difficulties in implementation.
[4] [1981] AC 578 at p 599H (Lord Dilhorne), pp 607F–608C (Lord Fraser of Tullybelton), pp 618H–619B (Lord Scarman), pp 627B–C (Lord Lane).
[5] *Pyx Granite Co v Ministry of Housing and Local Government* [1958] 1 QB 554.

Example

R v *Hillingdon BC ex p Royco Homes* [1974] 1 QB 720: A condition requiring that houses permitted by a permission should only be occupied by persons on the local authority's waiting list and that such occupiers should be given security of tenure for ten years was said to have been imposed in order to relieve the council's statutory obligations as a housing authority, and not to have been imposed for a planning purpose. (It should be noted, however, that in certain circumstances it can be appropriate to limit the occupation of houses to local people.)

2. Fairly and reasonably relate to the development permitted

Conditions imposed under section 72(1)(b) will, by their nature, relate directly to the development permitted by the permission. Conditions imposed under section 72(1)(a) have to be imposed **so far as it appears to the local planning authority to be expedient for the purposes of or in connection with the development authorised by the permission**. Again the test in *Newbury* merely describes the statutory position.

Whether a condition satisfies this test will depend entirely on the nature of the development permitted in any particular case. It is practically impossible to lay down general rules as to types of condition that will automatically fail this test.

Where a condition controls the use or operations to be carried out under the planning permission the test is plainly satisfied. A condition may, however, fairly and reasonably relate to the development permitted even though it seeks to police the use of existing facilities.

Examples

Penwith DC v *Secretary of State for the Environment* (1977) 34 P&CR 269: Planning permission was granted for a factory extension. Conditions restricting noise emissions from and hours of operation of the existing factory as well as the extension were held to be acceptable because the erection of the extension would permit the existing factory to be used more intensively. Thus the conditions related to the development permitted.

Peak Park Joint Planning Board v *Secretary of State for the Environment* [1980] JPL 114: Planning permission was granted for a new limestone quarry. It was held that conditions properly restricted the use of adjoining land already used as a quarry.

It is important that the relationship should be with the development covered by the planning permission. In *Newbury* itself, the development permitted by the permission was the temporary use of aircraft hangars. It was held that the Secretary of State was entitled to hold that a condition requiring the removal of the hangars after the use ceased did not relate to the development permitted—*i.e.* the use of the buildings. However, it was made clear that, in appropriate exceptional circumstances, it might be proper to impose such a condition in a planning permission permitting a change of use.

Other examples

Kember v *Secretary of State for the Environment and Tunbridge Wells BC* [1982] JPL 383: Planning permission was granted for a new dwelling with a condition limiting the occupation of an existing dwelling to an agricultural worker. It was held that because this condition was imposed in order to promote Green Belt policy generally, and was not related to the new building, it was invalid. Obviously conditions in permissions for new buildings can restrict the use of existing buildings (see above). This case illustrates the need to analyse the purpose of such a condition in each particular case.

Elmbridge BC v *Secretary of State for the Environment* [1989] JPL 277: A condition requiring obscure glazing did not fairly and reasonably relate to a proposal to alter an occupancy condition, unless there was something special about the new occupier that required obscure glazing.

Circular 11/95 also has a requirement that conditions must be relevant to the development permitted. In addition paragraphs 15–19 of the Annex impose a test based on necessity. This test requires the local planning authority to ask itself "whether planning permission would have to be refused if [the] condition were not to be imposed". This requirement is discussed further in Chapter 10. There is no legal requirement that conditions should be necessary in this sense.

3. Reasonable

This requirement is an application of the general principle of public law that the acts of public bodies must not be unreasonable[6]. The test of unreasonableness is high—a condition will only be unreasonable if no reasonable planning authority could have imposed it[7].

[6]*Associated Provincial Picture Houses Ltd* v *Wednesbury Corp* [1948] 1 KB 223.
[7]*Kingston–upon–Thames Royal BC* v *Secretary of State for the Environment* [1974] 1 All ER 193 at p 196g.

Other restrictions

In addition to these three tests conditions cannot require land to be dedicated to public use and cannot require the payment of money. All conditions also have to be certain.

1. Requiring the dedication of land for public purposes

A condition cannot require land to be given up for a public purpose. This restriction is designed to prevent conditions from being imposed to achieve ends that would normally require the payment of compensation. Thus, for example, a condition cannot require land to be provided for use as a highway (*Hall & Co v Shoreham–by–Sea UDC* [1964] 1 WLR 240). This restriction applies even though the land concerned is within the application site[8].

> *Other examples*
>
> *MJ Shanley* v *Secretary of State for the Environment* [1982] JPL 380: A condition requiring provision of 40 acres of open space for public use was invalid.
>
> *Westminster Renslade* v *Secretary of State for the Environment and Hounslow LBC* [1983] JPL 454: The judgment in this case contains dicta to the effect that a condition requiring provision of car parking spaces for public use would be unlawful.
>
> Contrast *Britannia (Cheltenham) Ltd* v *Secretary of State for the Environment* [1978] JPL 554 (upheld by the Court of Appeal at [1979] JPL 534): A condition requiring the provision of play areas and open space was acceptable because it did not require the land to be dedicated to public use.

2. Payment of money

In addition, a condition cannot require the payment of money. This is because any charge on the subject can only be imposed by clear parliamentary language. Thus a condition cannot require a payment towards the costs of providing infrastructure made necessary by the development. In addition, a condition cannot be imposed requiring a developer to provide security for the fulfilment of other conditions in a planning permission, or requiring a developer to enter into an agreement

[8]*City of Bradford Metropolitan Council* v *Secretary of State for the Environment* [1986] JPL 598, a case where it was said that a negative condition might have been acceptable.

with a local planning authority (which could, of course, require the payment of money).

In many instances it may be possible to circumvent this prohibition by an appropriate *Grampian* condition. A given proposal may only be acceptable if certain off site infrastructure works are carried out. The developer may be willing to fund such works if the permission he seeks is granted. While a *Grampian* condition could not lawfully prohibit development from commencing until such funding had been provided, it could prevent development from starting before the works themselves had been completed.

3. Certainty and enforceability

The approach of the courts to questions of lack of certainty in conditions is relaxed. A condition will be void only if it is so uncertain as to have no ascertainable meaning. The mere fact that it is ambiguous, may involve difficulties of construction, or may occasionally produce absurd results does not make it invalid[9]. Terms and phrases may be used in conditions if they have intelligible meanings, even though in particular cases it may be doubtful whether the term is applicable. The mere fact that difficulties may arise in ascertaining whether a condition has been infringed does not make it invalid[10].

> *Example*
>
> *Alderson* v *Secretary of State for the Environment* [1984] JPL 429: A condition requiring occupation by "person employed or last employed locally in agriculture" had an intelligible meaning, even though there might be cases where it was doubtful whether it applied.

A rare example of a condition invalid for uncertainty is provided by the decision in *MJ Shanley* v *Secretary of State for the Environment* [1982] JPL 380. In that case a condition required that local people should be offered the first opportunity to purchase the houses permitted by the permission. This was invalid as it was quite unclear how or on what terms this first opportunity was to be offered, and the condition would have been incapable of being enforced.

Practical difficulties in enforcement do not constitute a separate head of challenge[11].

[9]*Fawcett Properties Ltd* v *Buckinghamshire CC* [1961] AC 636, per Lord Denning at p 678.
[10]*Bizony* v *Secretary of State for the Environment* [1976] JPL 306.
[11]*Bromsgrove DC* v *Secretary of State for the Environment* [1988] JPL 257.

Land outside application site and outside applicant's control

Section 72(1)(a) makes it clear that a condition can regulate the development or use of land either if that land is **land in respect of which the application was made**, or if that land is **under the control of the applicant**.

A condition requiring action to be taken on land that is neither land "in respect of which the application is made", nor within the "control" of the applicant cannot be imposed[12].

1. Land under control of applicant

Whether "control" exists is a question of fact and degree. Control does not require ownership of the land. The test is whether the local planning authority can be satisfied that the applicant will be able to comply with any condition imposed on the relevant land.

> *Examples*
>
> *Wimpey* v *New Forest DC* (1979) 250 EG 249: "Control" does not require having an estate or interest in the land, but only such right as is needed to secure implementation of the condition. The Secretary of State was entitled to conclude that an agreement giving the developer a right of access over land was insufficient control for the purposes of a condition requiring that construction traffic should use the land for access to the site.
>
> *Augier* v *Secretary of State for the Environment* (1979) 38 P&CR 219: The Secretary of State was entitled to conclude that visibility splays would be provided on the basis of the landowner's willingness to sell the necessary land to the developer, and the developer's undertaking to make an agreement with the highway authority to provide the splays.

Adequacy of control has to be assessed at the time the decision on whether planning permission should be granted is made[13].

2. Land in respect of which application is made

The land **in respect of which the application is made** is the application site. Under the Town and Country Planning (Applications) Regulations 1988 applicants have to identify a specific area of land as the

---

[12]*Medina BC* v *Proberum Ltd* [1990] 3 PLR 79 at p 85E, *Mouchell Superannuation Trustees* v *Oxfordshire CC* [1992] 1 PLR 97.
[13]*Atkinson* v *Secretary of State for the Environment* [1983] JPL 599.

application site. It is invariably identified by a red line on a plan accompanying the application. There is no requirement that an applicant should have control (see above) over land within the application site: an applicant can apply for planning permission for land that he does not own. The applicant must notify the owners of such land within the application site when the application is made[14], but such owners do not have to consent to the application being made.

If planning permission is granted, conditions can regulate activities on any part of the application site, regardless of who controls it. A developer may know that a proposed development will not be permitted unless certain conditions can be imposed. These may relate to land he does not control. Provided that such land is included within the application site, the developer's lack of control will not matter. Of course, such a conditional planning permission, once granted, would not normally be capable of being implemented without the co-operation of the person with control of the relevant part of the application site.

However, if conditions are inappropriately worded, this may not be the case. In *Atkinson* v *Secretary of State for the Environment* [1983] JPL 599 planning permission was granted for the construction of seven houses subject to conditions requiring an existing building to be demolished, and a new access to be constructed. The application site included all the relevant land. However, by the time that the planning permission was granted the land over which the access had to be constructed, and on which the building to be demolished stood, had been sold off by the developer. The new houses were built, but the conditions were not complied with. It was held that an enforcement notice could be issued against the new owners of the relevant land requiring compliance with the conditions. It was pointed out by Woolf J that it would be unreasonable for a local planning authority to take enforcement action against a completely innocent owner of land subject to such a condition, and that normally the recipient of any such enforcement notice would be able to recover the expense of complying with it from the developer, by reason of what is now section 178(2) of the 1990 Act. Also, the notification requirements referred to above should normally alert a local planning authority to situations where land required for the satisfactory implementation of development is not within the applicant's control. Nevertheless extreme cases, like *Atkinson*, obviously do occur.

3. *Grampian* conditions

A positive condition attached to a permission for development on site A requiring works to be carried out on site B plainly relates to site B. If site

[14]Under Article 6 of the Town and Country Planning (General Development Procedure) Order 1995.

B is neither part of the application site nor within the control of the applicant, such a condition cannot be imposed. A *Grampian* condition stating that development of site A shall not be begun until works on site B have been completed regulates the development of site A. Site B does not have to be within the application site, nor within the applicant's control for such a condition to be imposed.

A *Grampian* condition can thus often be used to secure the grant of planning permission in situations where a developer does not control all the land needed to secure the satisfactory implementation of a development. As has been pointed out above, the decision in *British Railways Board* v *Secretary of State for the Environment and Hounslow LBC* [1993] JPL 342 means that there does not have to be a reasonable prospect that the relevant off site works will actually take place before a *Grampian* condition can lawfully be imposed. (It is, however, the Secretary of State's policy that such conditions should only be imposed if there is in fact a reasonable prospect of the requirement being carried out within the time for implementation of the permission[15].)

British Railways Board concerned a development which required access over land not within the applicant's control. This land was included within the application site. However, there is no reason to suppose that a *Grampian* condition can only be imposed if the application site includes the land on which the contingent event has to occur. As has been pointed out above, section 72 has no bearing on this question since a *Grampian* condition only "regulates" the development permitted by the permission.

Reasons

The local planning authority must give reasons for the imposition of any conditions[16]. However, failure to give reasons does not render the condition invalid[17].

Severance of invalid conditions

If a condition is found to be invalid as a matter of law, the entire planning permission will also be invalid unless the condition can be severed from the permission. If it can be so severed, only the condition will be quashed, leaving the remainder of the planning permission intact.

[15]Para 40 of Circular 11/95.
[16]Article 22(1)(a) of the General Development Procedure Order 1995.
[17]*Brayhead (Ascot)* v *Berkshire CC* [1964] 2 QB 303.

Whether a condition can be severed depends on whether it is fundamental to the planning permission[18]. "Fundamental" conditions cannot be severed. "Unimportant" or "incidental" conditions can, however, be severed[19].

It is not easy to ascertain precisely what is required before a condition can be regarded as fundamental to a planning permission. Conditions dealing with time limits on implementation and regulating important features of the permitted development have been regarded as fundamental. The occasions on which conditions have been regarded as severable are relatively rare.

Example: severable

R v *St Edmundsbury BC ex p Investors in Industry Commercial Properties Ltd* [1985] 3 All ER 234: A condition in a planning permission for a supermarket development which required independent retail outlets to be provided could be severed.

Examples: not severable

Hall & Co v *Shoreham–by–Sea UDC* [1964] 1 WLR 240: Condition requiring that an access road to serve the permitted development should be constructed and effectively dedicated to public use.

Kent CC v *Kingsway Investments (Kent) Ltd* [1971] AC 72: The House of Lords held (by a majority) that a condition stating that planning permission would lapse after three years unless reserved matters had been approved by then was fundamental and could not be severed.

R v *Hillingdon BC ex p Royco Homes* [1974] 1 QB 720: Condition requiring that houses in a housing development should only be occupied by persons on the council's waiting list.

Mouchell Superannuation Trustees v *Oxfordshire CC* [1992] 1 PLR 97: Condition in a planning permission for limestone extraction requiring that access to the site should be by a certain road which had to be improved to the county surveyor's satisfaction.

[18]*Hall & Co* v *Shoreham–by–Sea UDC* [1964] 1 WLR 240 per Hodson LJ; *Kent CC* v *Kingsway Investments (Kent) Ltd* [1971] AC 72 per Lord Morris of Borth–y–Gest; *R* v *Hillingdon BC ex p Royco Homes* [1974] 1 QB 720.
[19]*Hall & Co* v *Shoreham–by–Sea UDC* (above) per Pearson LJ; *Kent CC* v *Kingsway Investments (Kent) Ltd* (above) per Lord Morris of Borth–y–Gest.

Conditions which Amend the Application Scheme

CHAPTER 3

Conditions which Amend the Application Scheme

If planning permission is granted without the imposition of any conditions, it will permit whatever development was identified in the application. In fact all planning permissions for new development will have some conditions, if only the statutory conditions dealing with time limits on implementation (see Chap 4).

By limiting the extent of built development on site, or the way in which permitted activities are to be carried out, conditions can cut down what would otherwise be permitted by granting the application. This chapter discusses the extent to which conditions can alter the scope of the development identified in the original application.

This point has direct bearing on the question of amendments to submitted schemes. When faced with an application, a local planning authority can only grant planning permission for the development identified therein, or such modified development as can be achieved by the proper imposition of conditions. It is common for developers, once an application has been made, to suggest amendments to the application to overcome objections to the original scheme. Unless the amended scheme can be permitted by imposing conditions on the scheme identified in the application, a new application will need to be made.

It is often particularly important to know what amendments can be made to an original application by the imposition of conditions when the application is the subject of an appeal to the Secretary of State.

Enlarging the application scheme

The imposition of a condition cannot have the effect of permitting more development than was originally applied for. This applies to physical and time limits placed on the development in the application[1]. It follows that a condition cannot add features not embraced by the original application.

[1]*Cheshire CC v Secretary of State for the Environment and Rathbone* [1991] JPL 335.

Conditions will be construed so as not to permit the enlargement of the scope of the development.

> *Example*
>
> *Cadogan* v *Secretary of State for the Environment* [1993] JPL 664: A condition in a planning permission for mineral extraction stated that, prior to the start of development, the operators should carry out tests to demonstrate that sufficient water supply was available to allow lakes intended in a restoration scheme to be provided. The condition continued: "if the sufficiency of water supply cannot be demonstrated to the satisfaction of the mineral planning authority then an alternative restoration scheme shall be submitted to and agreed by the mineral planning authority". Although read literally this condition would permit the submission of a restoration scheme outside the scope of the original application, it was held that the condition should be construed as permitting only the submission of an alternative restoration scheme within the scope of the original application.

Reducing the scope of the application scheme

It is common for developers to come forward with amendments which reduce the scope of a scheme identified in an application. In *Bernard Wheatcroft* v *Secretary of State for the Environment* [1982] JPL 37 it was held that the Secretary of State had wrongly concluded that it was not open to him to grant planning permission for a scheme of 250 houses on 25 acres when the original application had sought planning permission for about 420 houses on 35 acres. Forbes J held that the correct approach was that a condition restricting the development to the smaller scheme could have been imposed provided it did not substantially alter the development for which permission was sought. The main criterion for assessing whether a revised scheme substantially differed from an original scheme was whether the change was such as to mean that those originally consulted needed to be consulted afresh on the revised scheme.

The test of "substantial difference" is one of fact and degree. However, the emphasis on whether consultees have been deprived of an opportunity to comment means that it will very often be possible to grant planning permission for a development that is simply less than that which was applied for[2].

[2] See dicta in *Wessex Regional Health Authority* v *Secretary of State for the Environment and Salisbury DC* [1984] JPL 344.

Other cases

Kent CC v *Secretary of State for the Environment* (1976) 33 P&CR 70: Planning permission was granted for an oil refinery subject to a condition preventing deliveries by road. Although deliveries by road had originally been contemplated, it was held that the imposition of this condition did not take away the substance of the planning permission granted. The position would have been different if the condition had made the planning permission unworkable.

Wadehurst Properties Ltd v *Secretary of State for the Environment and Wychavon DC* [1991] JPL 740: A decision that a smaller scheme was substantially different from the application scheme was quashed because the inspector had failed to explain why the difference in size meant that the smaller scheme was substantially different, and had not considered whether the by–passing of public consultation would have mattered.

CHAPTER 4

Conditions Imposing Time Limits

CHAPTER 4

Conditions Imposing Time Limits

Introduction

If planning permission for new buildings or a new use of land were granted without any conditions, the right to carry out the relevant development would exist indefinitely. A valid planning permission capable of implementation enures for the benefit of the land and cannot be abandoned by the conduct of a particular owner or occupier of the land[1]. The relevant development could start many years after the grant of planning permission. To prevent unimplemented planning permissions continuing to have legal force indefinitely conditions requiring development to be begun within certain time limits are imposed by statute.

Statutory time limits

The relevant provisions are sections 91 and 92 of the 1990 Act. Section 92 deals with outline planning permissions. As is pointed out in Chapter 1, an outline permission is a permission for the erection of a building, subject to condition(s) reserving for subsequent approval siting, design, external appearance, means of access or landscaping. Matters reserved for subsequent approval are known as "reserved matters". Subject to certain specified exceptions, section 91 deals with all other planning permissions.

Where section 91 or 92 applies, the relevant planning authority is directed by the Act to impose a time limit condition. If the planning authority ignores the Act, a time limit condition is deemed to have been imposed (see ss 92(3) and 91(3)). The deemed condition is:

1. *Outline permissions* Application for approval of reserved matters to be made within three years, and the development to be begun within five years, or within two years of the relevant approval, whichever is the later (s 92(2))
2. *Other planning permissions* Development to be begun within five years (s 91(3)).

[1]*Pioneer Aggregates Ltd* v *Secretary of State for the Environment* [1985] AC 132.

If the planning authority obeys the Act and imposes a time limit condition, that condition must be in the same form as those mentioned above; however, the authority has the discretion to impose different time periods (ss 92(4) and 91(1)(b)).

Where permissions not caught by sections 91 and 92 do have time limit conditions, there is special provision dealing with operations carried out after the limit has expired[2].

I. Section 91

Section 91(1)–(3) provides:

(1) Subject to the provisions of this Section, every planning permission granted or deemed to be granted shall be granted or, as the case may be, be deemed to be granted, subject to the condition that the development to which it relates must be begun not later than the expiration of—

  (a) five years beginning with the date on which the permission is granted, or, as the case may be, deemed to be granted; or

  (b) such other period (whether longer or shorter) beginning with that date as the authority concerned with the terms of the planning permission may direct.

(2) The period mentioned in subsection (1)(b) shall be a period which the authority consider appropriate having regard to the provisions of the development plan and to any other material considerations.

(3) If planning permission is granted without the condition required by subsection (1), it shall be deemed to have been granted subject to the condition that the development to which it relates must be begun not later than the expiration of five years beginning with the date of the grant.

Section 91(4) provides that these time limits do not apply to the following types of planning permission:

- Outline permissions (subs (4)(g))—these are covered by section 92
- Planning permission granted by a development order (subs (4)(a))—these permissions are generally available permanently
- Retrospective planning permission (subs (4)(b))—a time limit on implementation would usually be inappropriate for such permissions
- Planning permission granted for a limited period (subs (4)(c))

[2]Section 72(3) of the 1990 Act. This provides that where such a permission covers the carrying out of operations, and contains a condition that operations must be commenced before a specified time, operations commenced after that time do not constitute development for which that permission was granted.

- Certain mineral planning permissions (subs (4)(d))
- Planning permissions granted by enterprise zone schemes and simplified planning zone schemes (subs (4)(e) and (f)).

2. Section 92

Section 92(2)–(5) provides:

> (2) Subject to the following provisions of this Section, where outline planning permission is granted for development consisting in or including the carrying out of building or other operations, it shall be granted subject to conditions to the effect—
>
>> (a) that, in the case of any reserved matter, application for approval must be made not later than the expiration of three years beginning with the date of the grant of outline planning permission; and
>>
>> (b) that the development to which the permission relates must be begun not later than—
>>
>>> (i) the expiration of five years from the date of the grant of outline planning permission; or
>>>
>>> (ii) if later, the expiration of two years from the final approval of the reserved matters or, in the case of approval on different dates, the final approval of the last such matter to be approved.
>
> (3) If the outline planning permission is granted without the conditions required by subsection (2), it shall be deemed to have been granted subject to those conditions.
>
> (4) The authority concerned with the terms of an outline planning permission may, in applying subsection (2) substitute, or direct that there be substituted, for the periods of three years, five years or two years referred to in that subsection such other periods respectively (whether longer or shorter) as they consider appropriate.
>
> (5) They may also specify, or direct that there be specified, separate periods under paragraph (a) of subsection (2) in relation to separate parts of the development to which the planning permission relates; and, if they do so, the condition required by paragraph (b) of that subsection shall then be framed correspondingly by reference to those parts, instead of by reference to the development as a whole.

It is possible to make a number of alternative applications for approval of reserved matters, provided that they are all made within the time limit. The approval of reserved matters may be by the Secretary of State on appeal (see s 93(2)).

Subsection (6) provides that, in deciding whether to use their powers under subsections (4) and (5), local planning authorities shall have regard to the development plan and any other material considerations.

3. Consequences of non-compliance with time limit conditions

The consequences of failure to comply with a condition imposed by reason of section 91 or 92 are set out in section 93(4). This provides that:

(a) development carried out after the date by which the conditions require it to be carried out shall be treated as not authorised by the permission; and

(b) an application for approval of a reserved matter, if it is made after the date by which the conditions require it to be made, shall be treated as not made in accordance with the terms of the permission.

The carrying out of development not authorised by planning permission will amount to a breach of planning control against which enforcement action can be taken.

Even though an application for approval of reserved matters has not been made within the time limit imposed by the relevant condition this will not mean that the planning permission lapses. It may be possible to modify the time limit in the reserved matter condition so as to extend the time limit. This point is discussed further in Chapter 6.

A special procedure exists for seeking the renewal of expired planning permissions[3].

[3]See r 3 of the Town and Country Planning (Applications) Regs 1988.

Implementation of Planning Permission

CHAPTER 5

Implementation of Planning Permission

A grant of planning permission lapses if the development is not begun within the period specified in the time limit condition. Beginning the development "implements" the planning permission. Implementation means that the time limit condition is complied with, and the planning permission is no longer liable to lapse. The conditions in a planning permission only begin to bite once the permission has been implemented[1]. Once implemented, a planning permission remains alive indefinitely. It is therefore very important for developers faced with planning permissions that are about to lapse to know what works or activities are necessary to constitute implementation. In addition there may be cases where planning permissions which have not lapsed can no longer be implemented because of the effect of other development that has taken place in the meantime. Also, particular problems arise when developers attempt to implement planning permissions by carrying out works that breach other conditions. These questions are considered below.

Can a planning permission still be implemented?

1. Planning permission for operational development

Effect of subsequent operational development
A planning permission which has not lapsed may not be capable of implementation if subsequent development on the land makes such implementation impossible. In *Pilkington* v *Secretary of State for the Environment* [1973] 1 WLR 1257 planning permission was granted in 1953 for the construction of a bungalow. The application site included surrounding land which was to be a smallholding. In 1954 planning permission was granted for the construction of a bungalow on part of the previous application site. This bungalow was built. It was held that the 1953 planning permission was no longer capable of being implemented because the permission had contemplated the use of the entire remainder

[1]*Handoll* v *Warner Goodman Street* (1995) 25 EG 157.

of the application site as a smallholding, something which was no longer possible.

The approach in *Pilkington* is based on the physical impossibility of carrying out an earlier permission by reason of what has subsequently taken place on the land[2]. This approach was approved by the House of Lords in *Pioneer Aggregates Ltd* v *Secretary of State for the Environment* [1985] AC 132.

> **Example**
>
> *Wealdon DC* v *Taylor* [1992] 1 PLR 42: In 1987 planning permission was granted for the replacement of an existing dwelling with a new house to have a curtilage of 0.5 acres. In 1988 planning permission was granted for the replacement of the same existing dwelling with a different new house in a curtilage of 4.33 acres. The 1988 planning permission was implemented. The original dwelling was removed, but the new house did not stand on the 0.5 acre site identified in the 1987 planning permission. It was held that the 1987 planning permission could no longer be implemented because this permission related to the replacement of the original dwelling, something which had already happened.

Effect of subsequent change of use

Where the original planning permission is for operational development and the later, implemented planning permission is for a change of use, it is much less likely that the carrying out of the change of use will make the implementation of the operational development planning permission impossible.

> **Examples**
>
> *Durham CC* v *Secretary of State for the Environment* [1990] 1 PLR 103: In 1947 planning permission was granted for certain quarrying operations. Some quarrying was carried out. In 1957 planning permission was granted for a change of use to refuse tipping. Tipping was duly carried out. In 1986 the landowners sought to resume quarrying. The Court of Appeal held that the 1947 planning permission would permit this. The 1947 planning permission had, of course, been implemented when the initial quarrying took place. However, as the 1947 planning permission was for operational development, it remained in

---

[2]*Prestige Homes* v *Secretary of State for the Environment and Shepway DC* [1992] JPL 842.

existence for as long as the quarrying operations that it covered were being executed. This contrasts with a planning permission for a change of use which is spent as soon as the change occurs. There was nothing in the change of use that had occurred which meant that further mining operations covered by the 1947 planning permission were incapable of taking place.

McDonald's Restaurants Ltd v *Camden LBC* [1993] 1 PLR 57: Prior to 1987 premises were used as a restaurant. In 1987 planning permission was granted for the construction of a rear extension to the restaurant. Between 1988 and 1990 the premises were used as a bookshop. In 1991 it was sought to implement the 1988 permission. It was held that nothing in the change of use that had taken place between 1988 and 1990 meant that the 1987 planning permission for operational development could no longer take place.

2. Planning permission for change of use

The position where planning permission is granted for a change of use is much simpler. Provided that the land or building is capable of accommodating the new use the permission is still capable of being implemented. The fact that, in the period after the permission was granted, operations have taken place on the land, or changes of use have occurred, will not affect this.

What constitutes implementation?

1. Statutory provisions

Section 56(2)–(6) of the 1990 Act lays down what constitutes the commencement of development for the purpose of time limit conditions imposed by sections 91 and 92. Section 56(2) provides that development begins **on the earliest date on which any material operation comprised in the development begins to be carried out**.

Section 56(4) defines **material operation** as:

(a) **any work of construction in the course of the erection of a building;**
(aa) **any work of demolition of a building;**
(b) **the digging of a trench which is to contain the foundations, or part of the foundations, of a building;**
(c) **the laying of any underground main or pipe to the foundations, or part of the foundations, of a building or to any such trench as is mentioned in paragraph (b);**

   (d) any operation in the course of laying out or constructing a road or
      part of a road;
   (e) any change in the use of any land which constitutes material
      development.

Subsection (5) gives a definition of **material development**. This is considered below at page 41.

The drafting of section 56 is not particularly happy. It provides that a planning permission is implemented by carrying out a **material operation**, which includes a change of use (subs (4)(e)). This is unfortunate, because elsewhere in the 1990 Act operations and changes of use are treated as distinct concepts. The introduction of **material development** in subsection (4)(e) (a concept that applies only to changes of use) is also confusing.

Where planning permission is for operational development, subsection (4)(a)–(d) is relevant. Where such a permission also contemplates a change of use, subsection (4)(e) is also relevant. Where planning permission is for a change of use alone, only subsection (4)(e) applies.

2. Section 56(4)(a)–(d)—implementation by carrying out works

The terms of subsection (4)(a)–(d) make it obvious that works which constitute a relatively minor part of an entire scheme will be sufficient to implement a planning permission for building operations. Provided the works are not *de minimis*, there is no test based on the quantum of the works[3]. Works are not *de minimis* just because their cost is small[4].

The developer does not need to be firmly committed to carrying out the development covered by the planning permission, although such works must not be "colourable" and must be genuinely done for the purpose of carrying out the development[5].

Examples

Spackman v *Secretary of State for the Environment* [1977] 1 All ER 257: The partial construction of a soakaway and the laying of three trenches containing pipes implemented a planning permission even though the works were not in the location required by the planning permission. The developer intended that the works should be related to the planning permission, and the incorrect siting was the result of a mistake.

---

[3] *Thayer* v *Secretary of State for the Environment* [1992] JPL 264.
[4] *United Refineries Ltd* v *Essex CC* [1978] JPL 110.
[5] *Malvern Hills DC* v *Secretary of State for the Environment* [1982] JPL 439.

High Peaks BC v *Secretary of State for the Environment* [1981] JPL 366: The digging of a trench was sufficient to implement a planning permission even though the intention was not to proceed with the development at once, and the trench was later backfilled.

Hillingdon LBC v *Secretary of State for the Environment* [1990] JPL 575: Certain works were done to implement a planning permission for a hotel. The developer was not committed to carrying out the hotel development, which was not his preferred option for the site. However, it was held that an inspector was entitled to conclude that the hotel planning permission had been implemented on the basis that he was unable to say that "the development would not be built and therefore that the specified operation could not have been comprised in the development".

The works carried out must be related to the relevant planning permission[6]. Works which might otherwise implement a planning permission will not do so if they are related to some other development.

Examples

Handoll v *Warner Goodman Streat* (1995) 25 EG 157: Construction of a house 90 feet away from the location identified in the outline planning permission did not implement the permission, with the result that conditions in the permission did not bite.

South Oxfordshire DC v *Secretary of State for the Environment* [1981] JPL 359: The digging of trenches did not implement a planning permission because the trenches were related to a different development.

Oakimber v *Elmbridge BC* [1992] JPL 48: The change of use of land and the construction of certain roads was carried out in connection with the landowner's continuing activities and were not related to a planning permission for industrial development. The works therefore did not implement the planning permission.

[6]*Thayer* v *Secretary of State for the Environment* (see 3 above).

The particular problems of works intended to implement a planning permission that are in breach of condition are considered below.

3. Section 56(4)(e)—implementation by change of use
Any change in the use of the land that constitutes material development can implement a planning permission (subs (4)(e)). **Material development** means any development (other than development falling within certain excepted categories[7]) (s 56(5)). This is not a particularly enlightening provision. Given that the material development will have to be comprised in the development permitted (subs (2)), the practical consequence is that planning permission for a material change of use will, subject to the exceptions, be implemented by starting the use covered by the permission.

Purported implementation by works in breach of condition

What is required to satisfy a time limit condition and to implement a planning permission may be affected by other conditions in a planning permission. For example, a planning permission for housing development might contain a condition stating that no development shall take place until a landscaping scheme has been submitted to and approved by the local planning authority[8]. If, before such details are submitted to and approved by the local planning authority, the developer starts to construct the scheme, he will breach the condition. Do the works carried out in breach of condition implement the planning permission? Problems of this kind often occur in practice because compliance with conditions of this type often takes considerable time. If a period of inactivity follows the grant of planning permission, so that nothing is done until shortly before the time limit is about to expire, it may not be possible to carry out works that comply with all conditions of this type. On the other hand, if nothing is done the planning permission will lapse.

[7]Works carried out in order to comply with limitations in General Permitted Development Order permissions, certain categories of development involving houses that existed in 1948, and development specified in regulations made under s 56(5)(c). No such regulations have yet been made. However, certain forms of development do not count as "material operations" as a result of the Material Development Regulations 1967 (494). These include certain works associated with advertisements, recreation grounds, certain temporary works, changes between use classes in the 1963 Use Classes Order, certain uses and conversions of dwelling houses, certain industrial development and certain works associated with petroleum exploration, pipelines, and statutory undertakers.
[8]Model condition 25, Circular 11/95.

Section 56(2) provides that it is material operations **comprised in the development** that count as the start of development for the purpose of time limit conditions. This suggests that works that breach a condition in a planning permission would not implement the permission. This also seems to reflect the basic position in case law[9]. The law, however, is not entirely clear on this point.

As the case law on this subject has tended to be concerned with breaches of certain types of condition, it is sensible to consider these types separately.

1. Negative condition requiring approval of details

Conditions of the type mentioned above—*i.e.* that prevent any development from taking place until details of certain matters are submitted to and approved by the local planning authority[10]—are common for matters that are not reserved matters in outline planning permissions that are not outline planning permissions. (The special provisions for reserved matters in outline permissions are dealt with on page 45.)

If works are carried out that can properly be regarded as breaching such a condition, those works will not implement the permission[11].

The circumstances in which such a condition can properly be regarded as breached were considered in *Whitley (FG) & Sons Ltd* v *Secretary of State for Wales* (1993) 157 LGR 464. That case concerned a permission for mineral workings which contained a condition that stated:

> "No working shall take place except in accordance with a scheme to be agreed with the local planning authority or, failing agreement, as shall be determined by the Secretary of State, and such scheme shall among other matters include provision for
>
> (a) the order, direction, depth and method of working ..."

A further condition required that the development should be begun by 30 November 1978. In July 1977 details of the relevant matters were submitted to the local planning authority. The local planning authority did not grant approval, and an appeal to the Secretary of State was made

---

[9]See dicta in *Etheridge v Secretary of State for the Environment* [1984] JPL 340; *R v Elmbridge BC ex p Health Care Corp Ltd* [1992] JPL 39; *Oakimber v Elmbridge BC* [1992] JPL 48; *Staffordshire Moorlands DC v Secretary of State for the Environment* [1992] JPL 138; and *Whitley (FG) & Sons Ltd v Secretary of State for Wales* (1993) 157 LGR 464.
[10]E.g. model conditions 11, 17, 23, 28, 30, 32, 37, 40, 56, 58, 59, 64 and 73 in Circular 11/95.
[11]*Oakimber v Elmbridge BC*; *R v Elmbridge BC ex p Health Care Corp Ltd*; and *Whitley (FG) & Sons Ltd v Secretary of State for Wales* (*supra*, n9).

in November 1978. He eventually approved the details in May 1982. Works intended to implement the permission were carried out in November 1978. Work resumed on site in May 1983 and an enforcement notice was served against these works. By 1983 the November 1978 works were immune from enforcement action. However, the 1983 works were still liable to enforcement action unless the planning permission had been implemented by the 1978 works. The Court of Appeal held that these works had been effective to implement the planning permission even though the approvals required by the condition were not granted until after the works had started and after the deadline for implementation had passed.

The Court of Appeal based its decision on whether the works claimed to implement the planning permission were liable to enforcement action. Works that could be enforced against could not implement a planning permission.

In a situation where the works are carried out before the deadline, but before the approval of details, three situations fall to be considered.

Application made and approval granted before deadline
The court held that an approval granted after the works were carried out, but before the deadline for implementation, would protect the works from enforcement action provided that the works complied with the approval. Works so protected would be regarded as having implemented the permission. The protection arose because:

> "once the approval had been obtained, there would be no practical possibility of enforcement proceedings succeeding, since the results that the conditions were designed to achieve would have in fact have been achieved within the intended timescale." (p 469)

Application made before deadline, approval granted after deadline
In the circumstances of *Whitley* no approval had been granted before the deadline for implementation. Woolf LJ at p 469 said of the conditions:

> "Although the development had to be commenced by [30 November 1978], the condition did not expressly require the approval to be obtained by this date. There is however a clear implication that the developer will have applied for the approval before that date. As long as the developer has applied for that approval, I would not draw the implication that the approval had to be obtained by this date ... It must have been reasonably obvious to Parliament that there would be many situations where although a developer had made a timeous decision to apply for approval, that approval through no fault of the developer

could not be obtained until after the expiration of the time limits for implementing the permission. Where this happens and the developer had already implemented the permission by commencing operations pending the outcome of approval, it could be grossly unfair to the developer to regard him as being time barred. Indeed the operations which took place to comply with the time limit may be a matter which would not be affected by the terms of the approval although they would still contravene a blanket prohibition on the commencement of operations. Alternatively they might be of no significance from a planning point of view so no reasonable planning authority would contemplate enforcement action. I cannot accept that it was intended that in those circumstances a planning permission should be of no effect ..."

Woolf LJ proceeded to state that the test of whether or not the planning permission had been implemented should be tested "by examining the situation in an enforcement context by considering whether enforcement action is possible and if it is leaving the outcome to be determined in the enforcement proceedings" (p 469). The planning permission could therefore be regarded as implemented if, an application for approval having been made before the deadline, one of the following occurs after the deadline:

1. *Approval is granted before any enforcement action is taken* Woolf LJ seems to regard the later grant of approval as having retrospective effect in causing the earlier works to have implemented the permission. Thus once such approval is granted there ceases to be a breach of planning control. Such approval might, of course, only be granted on appeal.
2. *Approval is granted in enforcement proceedings* If an enforcement notice is served and the developer appeals, it is open to the Secretary of State to grant planning permission for the development enforced against. Woolf LJ said that "in the context of the enforcement proceedings the question of whether an approval, and if so what approval, should be given could be decided by the Secretary of State, the Secretary of State using if necessary his powers to grant a fresh planning permission" (p 468).

If approval is sought but ultimately refused, there will obviously not have been any implementation of the permission.

No application before deadline
If no application for approval of details is made before the deadline, there is no possibility of approval, retrospective or otherwise, being

granted. An application for approval made after the deadline for implementation would be invalid and a planning authority could not determine it. In this situation works carried out before the deadline would not be capable of implementing the permission.

Although Woolf LJ stated that, with the condition in *Whitley*, he would not draw the implication that the approval of details had to be obtained by the deadline for implementation because the condition did not expressly require this, there is plainly no practical difference between the condition in *Whitley* and a condition which requires that no development should take place until certain details have been submitted to and approved by the local planning authority. It would therefore seem that the above approach would apply to such conditions.

2. Reserved matters conditions in outline planning permissions

In the case of outline planning permissions the statutory condition deals expressly with the relationship between the obtaining approval of details and starting the development. Section 92(2)(b)(ii) provides that the development has to be begun within two years of the final approval of details (if this is more than five years after the grant of outline planning permission). The problem of a deadline for implementation falling before approval of details is granted therefore will not arise in the context of outline permissions.

Condition(s) in an outline planning permission will, of course, impose a time limit, based on the date of the permission, on the making of the application for approval of reserved matters.

If no application is made for the approval of details within the relevant time limit, it is possible to seek to vary the condition relating to the making of the application so as to extend the time limit, provided that the time for the commencement of development has not passed (*R v Secretary of State for the Environment ex p Corby DC* [1995] JPL 115, discussed in Chap 6).

3. *Grampian* conditions

A *Grampian* condition will require that development should not commence until a certain event, for example the provision of off–site infrastructure works, has occurred. Like the condition considered in *Whitley*, such a condition is negative in form. Unlike the condition in *Whitley*, it may not require any application to be made to the local planning authority. It could hardly be denied that works executed in an attempt to implement a planning permission, but in fact carried out before the relevant event has occurred, were in breach of such a condition. On this basis the better view is that such works would not implement the permission. This view is supported by dicta in *R v Elmbridge BC ex p Health Care Corp Ltd* [1992] JPL 39 and *Oakimber v Elmbridge BC* [1992] JPL 48. The whole force of a *Grampian* condition would, of course, be lost if the planning permission could be implemented before the relevant event took place.

4. Positive conditions

A positive condition may require that material operations should be carried out in a certain ways—*e.g.* certain aspects of the development must be carried out in accordance with an approved scheme. Material operations relied on to implement a planning permission may breach such a condition. Unlike the condition considered above, such a condition does not ban development from taking place until it is complied with. In *Clwyd CC v Secretary of State for the Environment* [1982] JPL 696 it was suggested that works in breach of a condition that was not a "condition precedent" could implement a planning permission[12]. Recent cases (especially *Whitley*)[13] have, however, revealed a marked hostility to an approach based on classifying conditions as "conditions precedent". The approach taken in these cases is that works that can properly be regarded as in breach of any condition are incapable of implementing a planning permission.

It should be noted that this kind of implementation problem will only arise if all the works carried out are in breach of the condition.

[12]This case went to the Court of Appeal *sub nom Welsh Aggregates Ltd* v *Secretary of State for Wales* [1983] JPL 50, but this point was not raised.
[13]See also *Etheridge v Secretary of State for the Environment*; *Oakimber v Elmbridge BC*; *R v Elmbridge BC ex p Health Care Corp Ltd*; *Staffordshire Moorlands DC v Secretary of State for the Environment* (*supra*, n9).

CHAPTER 6

Discharge of Conditions

CHAPTER 6

Discharge of Conditions

There are a number of ways in which a condition in a planning permission can be removed. If the condition is unlawful a legal challenge can be made. However, unless the condition is severable (see pages 23–24 above), the effect of a successful challenge to a condition will be that the entire planning permission is quashed.

In addition to the possibility of a legal challenge, there are avenues by which the planning merits of a condition can be challenged.

Section 78 appeal

A developer can appeal to the Secretary of State against the grant of a conditional planning permission under section 78(1)(a). The effect of such an appeal, however, is that the Secretary of State is entitled to deal with the appeal as if the original application for planning permission had been made to him in the first instance (s 79(1)). This means that it is open to the Secretary of State to refuse planning permission altogether.

Appeal against enforcement notice

If a developer breaches a condition and enforcement action is taken, an appeal can be made to the Secretary of State (s 174) (see Chap 8). It is open to the Secretary of State on such an appeal to grant planning permission for the development enforced against. Such planning permission can be subject to conditions. Where the basis of the enforcement action is breach of a condition the Secretary of State can discharge any conditions in an existing planning permission (s 177(1)(a) and (b)). Conversely, of course, it is always open to the Secretary of State to uphold the enforcement notice and to require the offending development to cease or be removed.

Retrospective planning permission without compliance with condition

Where development is carried out in breach of condition, it is possible to make an application for retrospective permission to permit the development without compliance with the condition (s 73A(1) and (2)(c)). This avenue is not available until the relevant development has been carried out. Carrying out development in breach of condition obviously involves risking enforcement action.

Section 73

It will be appreciated that none of these avenues is particularly attractive to a developer faced with a troublesome condition. There exists, in section 73, a method of challenge which is specifically designed to enable the merits of the conditions in a planning permission to be considered before the development is carried out without putting the entire planning permission at risk.

Section 73(1) permits **applications for planning permission for the development of land without complying with conditions subject to which a previous planning permission was granted**. Subsection (2) provides:

> On such an application the local planning authority shall consider only the question of the conditions subject to which planning permission should be granted, and—
>
> (a) if they decide that planning permission should be granted subject to conditions differing from those subject to which the previous permission was granted, or that it should be granted unconditionally, they shall grant planning permission accordingly, and
> (b) if they decide that planning permission should be granted subject to the same conditions as those subject to which the previous permission was granted, they shall refuse the application.

A section 73 application cannot be made **if the previous planning permission was granted subject to a condition as to the time within which the development was to be begun and that time has expired without the development having been begun** (subs (4)).

I. Nature of application
The application to remove or vary a condition is an application for planning permission.

An application under section 73, however, only seeks the removal or variation of conditions in a previous planning permission. Unlike a normal application for planning permission, the application does not have to be made on a standard form, but does have to comply with certain procedural requirements laid down in the Town and Country Planning (Applications) Regulations 1988. Regualtion 3 requires that such applications have to be made in writing and have to give sufficient information to enable the local planning authority to identify the previous grant of planning permission, and "any condition in question".

2. Determination of application

The particular feature of a section 73 application is that the local planning authority has to confine its attention to the conditions in the original planning permission. The original planning permission itself is not at risk. If that authority considers that the conditions in the original planning permission should be removed or changed, it can grant planning permission accordingly. It is open to that authority to impose new conditions that are more onerous than the ones that the developer wants to vary or remove. In theory the local planning authority can also rewrite the other conditions in the planning permission.

The decision-maker must consider whether the circumstances at the time of the decision justify the condition. It is not enough for him to conclude that the condition should be discharged because it was inappropriate at the time the permission was granted (see *Sevenoaks DC v Secretary of State for the Environment* [1995] JPL 126).

3. Appeals

The developer has the right to appeal against the local planning authority's decision to the Secretary of State (see s 78(1)). On an appeal the Secretary of State's powers are the same as those of the local planning authority (see s 79(4)). Thus he can only consider the conditions subject to which the original permission was granted. Like the local planning authority he can make them more onerous.

4. Scope of section 73

The power under section 73 only applies to planning permissions that have not lapsed (s 73(4)). If development has not been commenced within the time required for implementation, it is not possible to apply under section 73 to extend the period specified in the relevant time limit condition. A fresh grant of planning permission will be required.

In *R v Secretary of State for the Environment ex p Corby BC* [1995] JPL 115, the application of section 73 to outline planning permissions was considered. In that case outline permission had been granted subject to a condition requiring that an application for approval of details of reserved matters should be made within two years of the date of the permission and that the development should be commenced within four years of the date of the permission, or two years of the final approval of details of reserved matters, whichever was the later. The judgment was made on the basis that no application for approval of details was made within the two-year period. Shortly after this period had expired the developers applied to modify the conditions so as to extend the two-year period. The Secretary of State expressed the view that an application under section 73 could be made "at any time prior to the expiry of the period for beginning development". Pill J held that the only limit on the right to make a section 73 application was that contained in section 73(4) (namely that the development has not been begun within the appropriate time limit), and that that restriction was not applicable. As a result the section 73 application was valid.

Immunity from Enforcement Action

CHAPTER 7

Immunity from Enforcement Action

Introduction

Once a planning permission containing conditions is implemented, the conditions come into force, so as to be capable of being breached.

Failure to comply with a condition constitutes a **breach of planning control** (s 171A(1)(b)). When such breach occurs the local planning authority is entitled to take **enforcement action**, which may consist of issuing an **enforcement notice** and/or a **breach of condition notice** (s 171A(2)). In certain circumstances where an enforcement notice is served, a stop notice may also be served. Enforcement notices and stop notices are considered in Chapter 8, and breach of condition notices in Chapter 9.

In addition, a local planning authority may respond to a breach of planning control by seeking to obtain an **injunction** from the courts. Seeking an injunction does not constitute enforcement action within section 171A.

Government guidance on taking enforcement action is given in PPG 18.

Once a breach of planning control has occurred there are time limits on the taking of enforcement action. If enforcement action is not taken within these time limits the breach becomes immune from enforcement action, and the development is regarded as lawful.

Immunity from enforcement action

1. Section 171B
The immunity rules are set out in section 171B(1)–(3) of the 1990 Act. These provide:

> (1) Where there has been a breach of planning control consisting in the carrying out without planning permission of building, engineering, mining or other operations in, on, over or under land no enforcement action may be taken after the end of the period of

four years beginning with the date on which the operations were substantially completed.

(2) Where there has been a breach of planning control consisting in the change of use of any building to use as a single dwelling house, no enforcement action may be taken after the end of four years beginning with the date of the breach.

(3) In the case of any other breach of planning control, no enforcement action may be taken after the end of the period of ten years beginning with the date of the breach.

2. Breaches of condition

All breaches of condition fall within either subsection (2) or (3). Subsection (1) deals only with carrying out of operations **without planning permission**. Subsection (1) therefore does not apply where planning permission has been granted subject to conditions, and the operations are carried out in breach of those conditions.

It follows that the period for immunity for a breach of condition is ten years except where the breach of condition manifests itself in the change of use of a building to use as a single dwelling house, in which case the period before immunity is acquired is four years.

The four year rule set out in subsection (3) applies to the subdivision of a building into two or more separate dwellings, as well as the change of use of an entire building not previously in residential use to use as a single dwelling house[1].

If development carried out in breach of condition is immune from enforcement action by reason of the above provision, it counts as **lawful** development. A Certificate of Lawfulness of Existing Use or Development can be granted for such development under section 191.

3. Immunity acquired prior to 27 July 1992

Section 171B of the 1990 Act came into force on 27 July 1992. Prior to this date the immunity rules for breach of condition were different. In many instances it was more difficult to acquire immunity. However, there were some circumstances where a breach of condition acquired immunity after only four years where the same breach is now subject to the ten-year period. Section 4(2) of the Planning and Compensation Act 1991 and Article 5 of the Commencement Order provide that where, by 27 July 1992, a breach of planning control had become immune from enforcement action under the old rules, such immunity survives the coming into force of section 171B.

[1] *Van Dyke* v *Secretary of State for the Environment* [1993] JPL 564.

Cases may still arise where it is necessary to establish whether a breach of condition that has not acquired immunity under the new ten year rule had acquired immunity by 27 July 1992 under the old rules.

The old immunity rules were laid down in section 172 (now repealed) of the 1990 Act. There was no ten year rule at all in the old section 172. It provided that a breach of planning control was immune from enforcement action if it began before the end of 1963, unless the breach fell within section 172(4), in which case the period for immunity was four years. Section 172(4) covered:

(a) the carrying out without planning permission of building, engineering, mining or other operations in, on, over or under land; or
(b) the failure to comply with any condition or limitation which relates to the carrying out of such operations and subject to which planning permission was granted for the development of that land; or
(c) the making without planning permission of a change of use of any building to use as a single dwelling house; or
(d) the failure to comply with a condition which prohibits or has the effect of preventing a change of use of a building to use as a single dwelling house.

Breaches of condition within the old subsection (4)(d) benefit from the four-year immunity period under the new regime. However, breaches of condition falling within the old subsection (4)(b) do not. Breaches of this kind which started before 27 July 1988 but which have not continued for ten years will be immune under the old rules but not under the new rules. The scope of the old section 172(4)(b) is therefore still a matter of importance.

4. Scope of section 172(4)(b) (repealed)

Where planning permission is granted for the carrying out of building etc operations, and conditions relate directly to the operations themselves (*e.g.* conditions regulating how the building works are to be carried out), these are plainly caught by section 172(4)(b).

Conditions in such permissions may relate to how the completed building or existing buildings are to be used. There are two leading authorises on such conditions.

> *Harvey* v *Secretary of State for Wales* [1990] JPL 420: Planning permission was granted for a new farmhouse subject to a condition requiring that an existing farmhouse should either be demolished or put to an agricultural use (although not as a dwelling house) within one month of beneficial use of the new

farmhouse beginning. The Court of Appeal held that this condition did relate to the carrying out of building operations and so benefited from the four year rule. It was said that the condition related to the operational development involved in constructing the new farmhouse, and that this was sufficient. It was not necessary that the condition itself should require operational development to be carried out for it to fall within subsection (4)(b).

Newbury DC v *Secretary of State for the Environment* [1994] JPL 137: Planning permission was granted for a farmhouse subject to an agricultural occupancy condition. The Court of Appeal held that this condition did not relate to the carrying out of building operations, so that the four year immunity rule did not apply. The court distinguished *Harvey* on the basis that the condition there did not relate exclusively to occupancy but was related to the operation of demolishing the existing farmhouse. It also related to the carrying out of the building operations which brought into existence the new farmhouse. The occupancy aspect of the condition was merely a corollary to the requirement to demolish.

On the strength of *Newbury* it is clear that ordinary occupancy conditions imposed on permissions for new buildings do not have the benefit of the old four year rule. Conditions in permissions for the construction of new buildings which require the demolition of existing buildings plainly do have the benefit of the four year rule.

Where the permission is for a change of use, it is still possible to have a breach falling within section 172(4)(b). In *Kings Lynn BC* v *Secretary of State for the Environment and Smith* [1995] JPL 730 a condition in a planning permission for the conversion of a chapel to residential use required that, prior to occupation of the premises, an access should be laid out. It was held that failure to comply with this condition fell within section 172(4)(b) because the condition contained an express reference to the carrying out of operations.

The problem of breaches of condition which are immune under the old rules but not under the new rules will, of course, diminish with the passage of time.

5. Effect of previous enforcement action

Section 171B(4)(b) provides that the immunity rules in subsections (1)–(3) do not prevent:

> taking further enforcement action in respect of any breach of planning control if, during the period of four years ending with that action being taken, the local planning authority have taken or purported to take enforcement action in respect of the breach.

This means that if enforcement action is taken against a breach of planning control before the immunity period has expired, but the action is unsuccessful (with the result that the breach continues) the local planning authority can take further enforcement action within a four-year period. Indeed, if the second attempt at enforcement action is also unsuccessful, the local planning authority has a further four years to take action, and so on. The breach will not acquire immunity by continuing after the first enforcement action has taken place.

The initial enforcement action can include "purported" enforcement action. This includes issuing defective enforcement notices which have to be withdrawn (under section 173A) or which are quashed on appeal for technical reasons.

Section 171B(4)(b) is, of course, not relevant where the initial enforcement notice is properly issued but is quashed on appeal because planning permission is granted for the breach, or because the activity enforced against is already immune. There would be no question of taking further enforcement action in these instances.

Because in many instances the immunity rules became less favourable to local planning authorities on 27 July 1992, many enforcement notices were served shortly before that date. There may still be instances where these notices were unsuccessful and the local planning authority wishes to rely on subsection (4)(b) to take further enforcement action. Where this happens, the relevant immunity period is assessed on the basis of the new rules by reference to the date of the original enforcement action[2].

[2]*William Boyer (Transport) Ltd* v *Secretary of State for the Environment* [1994] EGCS 199.

CHAPTER 8

Enforcement Notices and Stop Notices

CHAPTER 8

Enforcement Notices and Stop Notices

Introduction

The most common method of taking action against a breach of planning control, including a breach of condition, is by serving an enforcement notice. An enforcement notice is an instruction from the local planning authority that a breach of planning control should be remedied within a certain time. There exists a right of appeal against an enforcement notice to the Secretary of State. The requirements of an enforcement notice are suspended while any such appeal is being determined.

If a local planning authority wishes to stop the carrying out of activity in breach of planning control while an enforcement notice is suspended pending an appeal, or in the period of time before an enforcement notice comes into effect, it can serve a stop notice. A stop notice is an instruction that the offending activity must cease more or less immediately.

Failure to comply with the requirements of an enforcement or a stop notice involves commission of a criminal offence.

Power to issue enforcement notices

The power to serve enforcement notices is conferred by section 172 of the 1990 Act. Subsection (1) provides that a local planning authority may issue an enforcement notice

> ... where it appears to them
> (a) that there has been a breach of planning control; and
> (b) that it is expedient to issue the Notice having regard to the provisions of the development plan and to any other material considerations.

The local planning authority must be able to show that, at the time it decided to issue the notice, there was a breach of planning control apparent to it.

Where a breach of planning control has occurred, a local planning authority has a discretion whether or not to take any action: it must decide that it is **expedient** to take action. The wide wording of section 172(1)(b) makes the exercise of this discretion difficult to challenge. However, a decision not to take enforcement action may be challenged if it is founded on an error of law[1] or is arbitrary or capricious[2].

Guidance on taking enforcement action is given in PPG 18. Paragraphs 8 and 9 deal with development in breach of planning control which could be made acceptable by the imposition of conditions.

Contents of enforcement notices

An enforcement notice must state the following matters under section 173 of the 1990 Act.

1. Section 173(1)—The matters which appear to the local planning authority to constitute the breach of planning control, and the paragraph in section 171A(1) within which, in the opinion of the local planning authority, the breach falls

Section 171A(1) categorises breaches of planning control as either **carrying out development without the required planning permission** or **failing to comply with any condition or limitation subject to which planning permission has been granted**. The local planning authority has to identify one of these categories.

Section 173(2) provides that a notice satisfies the requirement to state the matters alleged to constitute the breach of planning control **if it enables any person on whom a copy of it is served to know what those matters are**.

In addition the Secretary of State on an appeal has power to correct any defect, error or misdescription in an enforcement notice (s 176(1)(a)). It follows that defects in the description of the offending development are normally dealt with by an appeal to the Secretary of State. However, an enforcement notice will be a nullity if the allegations that it makes are not supported at all by the facts.

2. Section 173(3)—The steps which the authority requires to be taken and the activities which the authority requires to cease

The steps required by the enforcement notice must be imposed for one or more of the purposes set out in subsection (4), namely:

[1] *R v Secretary of State for the Environment ex p Hillingdon LBC* [1986] 1 All ER 810.
[2] *Perry v Stanborough (Development) Ltd* (1977) 244 EG 551.

(a) remedying the breach by making the development comply with the terms (including conditions and limitations) of any planning permission which has been granted in respect of the land, by discontinuing any use of the land or by restoring the land to its condition before the breach took place; or

(b) remedying any injury to amenity which has been caused by the breach.

In the case of a breach of condition the most likely steps will be ones designed to make the development comply with the condition. However, steps to achieve any of the purposes mentioned in subsection (4) may be appropriate.

Subsection (5) gives examples of what enforcement notices can require. These examples include:

(a) the alteration of any buildings or works;

(b) the carrying out of any building or other operations;

(c) any activity on the land not to be carried on except to the extent specified in the notice ...

Vague requirements

An appeal can be made against an enforcement notice on the grounds that the steps imposed are excessive. Most challenges to the steps imposed by enforcement notices are dealt with by such appeals. However, if the steps are sufficiently vague the notice will be a nullity. The test is whether the notice is hopelessly ambiguous so that the recipient cannot, for example, tell with reasonable certainty what steps he has to take to remedy the alleged breaches[3].

The mere fact that the steps imposed mean that situations may arise where it is doubtful whether they have been complied with does not make the notice a nullity[4].

Although the requirements of an enforcement notice may not have been challenged either in the civil courts or by way of an appeal to the Secretary of State, it may be possible to allege in criminal proceedings that they are too uncertain. In *Warrington BC* v *Garvey* [1988] JPL 752 it was suggested (in a direction to a jury) that in criminal proceedings a strict approach would be taken to assessing the precision of an enforcement notice. However, it is unclear what this might mean in practice: the two enforcement notices in that case were hopelessly defective (one alleged failure to comply with a condition in a planning permission but failed to identify the relevant condition, and the other failed to identify the land to which it related).

[3] *Hounslow LBC* v *Secretary of State for the Environment* [1981] JPL 510.
[4] *Ivory* v *Secretary of State for the Environment* [1985] JPL 796.

Under enforcement

The local planning authority has a discretion to under enforce. Thus the steps that it imposes in the enforcement notice do not have to ensure that all aspects of the breach of planning control should cease or be removed. Where a local planning authority chooses to under enforce, planning permission is treated as having been granted for those aspects of the development that could have been enforced against, but were not (subs (11)).

The Mansi *principle*

The requirements of an enforcement notice must not go beyond what is necessary to remedy the breach of planning control. In particular they must not take away lawful use rights, a point established in *Mansi* v *Elstree RDC* (1964) 16 P&CR 153. The Secretary of State will modify enforcement notices on appeal to ensure that this is so.

Relaxation of requirements

Under section 173A the local planning authority can waive or relax any requirement in an enforcement notice.

3. Section 173(8)—The date on which the enforcement notice is to take effect

The enforcement notice cannot take effect less than 28 days after it is served (s 172(3)(b)). It is during this period between service and taking effect that any appeal to the Secretary of State has to be made (see pages 66 *et seq* below). The period for compliance with the requirements of the notice does not begin to run until the notice has come into effect.

4. Section 173(9)—The period at the end of which any steps are required to have been taken or any activities to have ceased

A single enforcement notice can impose a series of requirements needed to remedy the breach of planning control, and can impose different time limits for different steps.

Under section 173A the local planning authority can extend any period for compliance in any enforcement notice it has issued.

5. Other requirements

Two other requirements for the contents of enforcement notices are imposed by regulation 3 of the Town and Country Planning (Enforcement Notices and Appeals) Regulations 1992, which are made under section 173(10), namely:

- the reasons for issuing the enforcement notice; and
- the precise boundaries of the land to which the notice relates, whether by reference to a plan or otherwise.

In addition regulation 4 requires an enforcement notice to be accompanied by an explanatory note setting out the rights of appeal to the Secretary of State.

Service of enforcement notices

Section 172(2) provides that a copy of the enforcement notice shall be served:

(a) **on the owner and on the occupier of the land to which it relates; and**

(b) **on any other person having an interest in the land, being an interest which, in the opinion of the authority, is materially affected by the notice.**

Owner is defined by section 336 of the Act as:

a person other than a mortgagee not in possession who, whether in his own right or as a trustee for any other person, is entitled to receive the rack rent of the land, or, where the land is not let at a rack rent, would be so entitled if it were so let.

Whether someone is an **occupier** is a question of fact and degree. Occupiers obviously include those with a legal right to occupy land. The term may also embrace licensees, for example if their occupation is exclusive and not transient[5]. In *Scarborough BC* v *Adams* [1983] JPL 673 the occupants of caravans parked in a layby were held to be occupiers within section 172(2).

The local planning authority has no discretion about serving owners and occupiers.

Section 329 of the Act makes provision for the service of notices where the identities of intended recipients cannot be identified. In summary the procedure is that, where the identity of an owner, occupier or person having an interest in the land cannot be ascertained after reasonable inquiry, an enforcement notice can be served by addressing it to such person either by name, or as "owner" or "occupier" of the premises (describing them), and then delivering it to some person on the premises, or affixing it conspicuously to some object on those premises (s 329(2)).

[5]*Stevens* v *Bromley LBC* [1972] 1 Ch 400.

Section 329(3) makes provision for the service of notices on occupiers and those with interests in land where it appears that land is unoccupied. In this case also notices can be affixed conspicuously to some object on the land.

Failure to serve an enforcement notice in accordance with the above provisions is a ground for appealing to the Secretary of State. In some circumstances the fact that an enforcement notice was not served can be a defence to criminal proceedings (see page 76 below).

Variation and withdrawal of enforcement notices

By section 173A, a local planning authority may withdraw an enforcement notice, or waive or relax any requirement in an enforcement notice, and, in particular, extend the period for compliance (subs (1)) whether or not the notice has taken effect (subs (2)). The local planning authority must give notice of any such withdrawal or relaxation to every person who was served with the enforcement notice (subs (3)).

If the effect of such relaxation is that the local planning authority is under enforcing (see page 64 above), that part of the offending development which is not enforced against is treated as having been granted planning permission (s 173(11)). However, if an enforcement notice is withdrawn completely, the local planning authority retains the power to take fresh enforcement action against the same beach of planning control in the future (s 173A(4)).

Appeals to the Secretary of State

There exists a right of appeal against an enforcement notice to the Secretary of State. On an appeal the Secretary of State can uphold the notice, whether in its original or in a varied form, or he can quash it. If the notice is quashed the Secretary of State may grant planning permission for the development enforced against.

1. Who may appeal
An enforcement notice binds the land, rather than particular individuals. As a result the categories of person who may appeal against the notice are wide, and are not confined to those served with it.

Any person with an **interest in the land** or who is a **relevant occupier** can appeal against an enforcement notice, whether or not the notice was served on that person (s 174(1)). A **relevant occupier** is a person who occupies the land by reason of a licence in writing both at the time of the issuing of the notice and at the time that the appeal is made (s 174(6)). It is possible that an occupier for the purposes of service (see page 65 above) may not be a relevant occupier for the purposes of an appeal. A trespasser has no right of appeal.

2. Time for appealing

Any appeal must be made before the enforcement notice comes into effect (s 174(3)). Section 172(3)(b) means that the notice has to be served at least 28 days before it comes into effect so as to ensure that recipients have adequate time to mount an appeal.

The time limit is absolute and the Secretary of State has no jurisdiction to accept late appeals[6].

3. Suspension of enforcement notice pending determination of appeal

The requirements of the enforcement notice are suspended while such an appeal is being determined (s 75(4)). An appeal by one person suspends the notice in its entirety—*i.e.* it is suspended as against all those interested in the land, not just the appellant.

4. Grounds of appeal

Section 174(2) sets out the only grounds on which an appeal can be made against an enforcement notice. An appellant has to specify which of the grounds form the basis of his appeal. The grounds are as follows.

Ground (a) **That in respect of any breach of planning control which may be constituted by the matters stated in the notice, planning permission ought to be granted or, as the case may be, the condition or limitation ought to be discharged**

This ground requests the Secretary of State to grant planning permission for whatever breach of planning control may have occurred, or to discharge any condition that may have been breached.

Quite apart from this ground of appeal, any appeal against an enforcement notice is deemed to involve making an application for planning permission for the matters alleged to constitute a breach of planning control (s 177(5)).

[6]*Howard v Secretary of State for the Environment* [1975] QB 235; *R v Secretary of State for the Environment ex p JBI Financial Consultants* [1989] JPL 365.

Ground (b) **That those matters have not occurred**

This ground is applicable when it is contended that the events alleged to constitute the breach of planning control have not occurred. It should not be raised when it is accepted that the events have occurred, but it is contended that they do not amount to a breach.

Ground (c) **That those matters (if they occurred) do not constitute a breach of planning control**

This ground is applicable when it is contended that the events alleged do not constitute a breach of condition or other breach of planning control.

Ground (d) **That, at the date when the notice was issued, no enforcement action could be taken in respect of any breach of planning control which may be constituted by those matters**

This ground is applicable when it is claimed that the alleged breach of planning control is immune from enforcement control by reason of effluxion of time.

Ground (e) **That copies of the enforcement notice were not served as required by section 172**

An enforcement notice should be quashed if it has not been properly served unless the failure to serve has not substantially prejudiced either the appellant or the person who was not correctly served (s 176(5)). In this event the Secretary of State may disregard the defective service.

Ground (f) **That the steps required by the notice to be taken, or the activities required by the notice to cease, exceed what is necessary to remedy and breach of planning control which may be constituted by those matters or, as the case may be, to remedy any injury to amenity which has been caused by any such breach**

Ground (g) **That any period specified in the notice in accordance with section 173(9) falls short of what should reasonably be allowed**

Grounds (f) and (g) do not go to the validity of the enforcement notice. If an appeal is allowed on these grounds the Secretary of State will insert what he considers to be appropriate terms.

5. Secretary of State's power of variation

By section 176(1), on an appeal under section 174 the Secretary of State may:

(a) correct any defect, error or misdescription in the enforcement notice; or

    (b) **vary the terms of the enforcement notice, if he is satisfied that the correction or variation will not cause injustice to the appellant or the local planning authority.**

This power can be used to make corrections to the description of the events alleged to have taken place, or to the description of the breach of planning control alleged to have taken place.

The power to vary the terms of the enforcement notice may involve the Secretary of State in cutting down the requirements of the notice (for example, to preserve existing use rights under the *Mansi* doctrine), or to specify a different method of remedying the breach of planning control.

The power under section 176(1) can only be exercised if the Secretary of State is satisfied that no injustice to either party to the appeal will be caused. As a result he must not correct something that goes to the substance of the matter[7].

6. Secretary of State's power to grant planning permission/ discharge or modify conditions on an enforcement notice appeal

Under section 177(1) the Secretary of State, on an enforcement notice appeal, can grant planning permission for any or all of the matters alleged to constitute a breach of planning control in respect of any or all of the land affected by the notice, and can discharge any condition or limitation subject to which planning permission was originally granted.

Grant of planning permission

The planning permission that the Secretary of State can grant is any planning permission that can be granted under Part III of the 1990 Act (s 177(3)). It thus includes planning permission to retain existing development without complying with conditions previously imposed (s 73A) and a planning permission subject to conditions under section 70. There is no right of appeal against any conditions imposed by the Secretary of State.

The Secretary of State's power to grant planning permission is confined to the matters covered by the enforcement notice[8]. The Secretary of State therefore cannot grant planning permission for any development that has not already taken place.

The Secretary of State's power to grant planning permission for development caught by the enforcement notice arises whether or not an appeal on ground (a) of section 174(2) has been made. This is because, by section 177(5), whenever an appeal is made against an enforcement

---

[7]*Miller Mead* v *Minister of Housing and Local Government* [1963] 2 QB 196.
[8]*Richmond–upon–Thames LBC* v *Secretary of State for the Environment* (1972) 224 EG 1555.

notice an application for planning permission for the offending development is deemed to have been made.

Discharge or modification of condition
When the Secretary of State decides to discharge an existing condition or limitation, he can substitute another condition or limitation, whether more or less onerous (s 177(4)).

Determination that development is lawful
In addition to granting planning permission for offending development, and modifying or discharging existing condition, the Secretary of State can determine that, at the date of the appeal, a particular use of land or breach of condition or particular operations on land were immune from enforcement action by reason of effluxion of time. If he so determines he can issue the appropriate Certificate of Lawfulness of Existing Use or Development.

Effect of enforcement notice and of subsequent grant of planning permission

Compliance with an enforcement notice does not discharge the notice (s 181(1)). Thus, a requirement in an enforcement notice that a use of land shall be discontinued means that the use must be discontinued permanently (s 181(2)). If such a use is discontinued, but later resumed, the later resumption will be in breach of the notice. Likewise if a building is removed or altered to comply with an enforcement notice, any later restoration of the building will be in breach of the notice (s 181(3)).

The only way to escape the effects of a valid enforcement notice is to obtain planning permission for the offending development. Section 180(1) provides that:

> where, after service of ... an Enforcement Notice ... planning permission is granted for any development carried out before the grant of that permission, the Notice shall cease to have effect to the extent that it is inconsistent with that permission.

Criminal liability for any previous failure to comply with the notice is, however, unaffected by this provision (s 180(3)).

Stop notices

A considerable period of time may elapse before an enforcement notice is capable of being breached. An enforcement notice cannot be breached until the period for compliance has expired. The period for compliance does not even begin to run until the enforcement notice has come into effect. At the very minimum the enforcement notice will not take effect until at least 28 days after service (s 172(3)(b)). If an appeal is made, the enforcement notice will not come into effect, if at all, until after the appeal is determined. It follows that an enforcement notice may be a fairly leisurely way to achieve the ending of a breach of planning control.

In situations where a speedy remedy is required a local planning authority can serve a **stop notice**. A stop notice can require the immediate cessation of any activity (known as **relevant activity**) prohibited by an enforcement notice. A stop notice depends on there being an enforcement notice, and only has effect to ban the relevant activity until the period for compliance in the relevant enforcement notice expires or the enforcement notice is quashed or withdrawn. In some circumstances, where a stop notice has been served and the relevant enforcement notice is later quashed or withdrawn, there is a liability to pay compensation.

Failure to comply with a stop notice constitutes a criminal offence. Guidance on the use of stop notices is given in Circular 21/91.

1. Relevant activity
A stop notice can only prohibit the carrying out of a **relevant activity** (s 183(1)). This is defined in section 183(2) as **any activity specified in the enforcement notice as an activity which the local planning authority require to cease and any activity carried out as part of that activity or associated with that activity**. Relevant activity can therefore embrace the carrying out of a use, or the carrying out of operations. Either could involve a breach of condition. A stop notice cannot be used to require the removal of built development that has already been constructed. The relevant activity must be one that is caught by the relevant enforcement notice, or associated with such an activity.

The prohibition in the stop notice can relate to all the land covered by the enforcement notice, or such part of that land as is specified in the stop notice (s 183(1)).

2. Exceptions
There are two activities that cannot be stopped by a stop notice:

1. the use of any building as a dwelling house (s 183(4));
2. any activity ... carried out (whether continuously or not) for a period of four years (s 184(5)). The period is calculated back from the date of service of the stop notice, and excludes any period during which the activity was authorised by planning

permission. This exclusion does not apply to activity associated with **building, engineering, mining or other operations, or the deposit of refuse or waste materials** (s 183(5A)).

If such an activity is caught by a stop notice, the notice is not void, but the recipient is entitled to disregard the notice so far as it covers such activity[9].

3. Power to serve a stop notice

A local planning authority may serve a stop notice if it considers it **expedient that any relevant activity should cease before the expiry of the period for compliance with an enforcement notice** (s 183(1)).

4. Effect of a stop notice

A stop notice may be served at the same time as the service of the relevant enforcement notice, or afterwards (s 183(1)), but not after the enforcement notice has taken effect (s 183(3)).

The stop notice itself must have a date on which it takes effect. That date must not be less than three days[10] nor more than 28 days from the date of service. The prohibition on the relevant activity starts when the stop notice takes effect (s 183(4)). The effect of a stop notice is therefore a speedy ban on the offending activity. Failure to comply with a stop notice is a criminal offence (see page 76 below).

There is no right of appeal against a stop notice, and a stop notice is not suspended if the relevant enforcement notice is appealed.

A stop notice is not invalid if the relevant enforcement notice was not served properly **if it is shown that the local planning authority took all such steps as were reasonably practicable to effect proper service** (s 184(8)).

5. Cessation of effect

Section 184(4) provides that a stop notice ceases to have effect when:

(a) the enforcement notice to which it relates is withdrawn or quashed; or
(b) the period for compliance with the enforcement notice expires; or
(c) notice of withdrawal of the stop notice is given under section 183(7).

If the enforcement notice on which the stop notice is based is withdrawn or quashed there is no reason for the stop notice to continue. When the

[9] *R v Epping Forest DC ex p Strandmill Ltd* [1990] JPL 415.
[10] Unless there are special reasons for greater urgency, in which case the local planning authority must state what these are (s 184(3)).

period for compliance with the enforcement notice expires the continuation of the relevant activity will constitute a breach of the enforcement notice itself, so again there is no reason for the stop notice to continue.

The local planning authority can withdraw a stop notice at any time by serving notice to that effect on those served with the original notice (s 183(7)).

6. Service of stop notice

A stop notice may be served by the local planning authority **on any person who appears to them to have an interest in the land or to be engaged in an activity prohibited by the notice** (s 183(6)). There are no categories of person who have to be served. The recipients of a stop notice are a matter for the local planning authority's discretion.

The provisions in section 329 concerning service of notices on persons whose identities cannot be ascertained (discussed at pages 65–66 above) apply to the service of stop notices.

Where a stop notice has been served, the local planning authority can also display a site notice stating that a stop notice has been served and giving details of the notice, including when it takes effect (s 184(6)). The effect of a site notice is to extend possible criminal liability: if a site notice has been displayed a person carrying on an activity in breach of the stop notice commits an offence even though the stop notice has not been served on him (s 187(1)).

7. Form of stop notice

There is no prescribed form for stop notices. However, a stop notice must refer to, and have attached to it a copy of, the relevant enforcement notice (s 184(1)). It must also specify the date on which it is to come into effect (s 184(2)).

8. Compensation

There are a number of circumstances in which the service of a stop notice can lead to a liability to pay compensation. These are set out in section 186(1), namely:

(a) **the enforcement notice is quashed on grounds other than those mentioned in paragraph (a) of Section 174(2);**
(b) **the enforcement notice is varied (otherwise than on the grounds mentioned in that paragraph) so that any activity the carrying out of which is prohibited by the stop notice ceases to be a relevant activity;**

> (c) the enforcement notice is withdrawn by the local planning authority otherwise than in consequence of the grant by them of planning permission for the development to which the notice relates; or
>
> (d) the stop notice is withdrawn.

Section 174(2)(a) covers the quashing of enforcement notices on the ground that planning permission should be granted for the activity enforced against. Compensation is thus awarded when the stop notice itself is withdrawn, or the relevant enforcement notice is withdrawn or quashed for reasons other than the grant of planning permission for the offending activity. This will cover situations where enforcement action should not have been taken (because the activities enforced against were immune from enforcement action, did not constitute a breach of planning control, or did not take place) or where the enforcement action was defective (because the enforcement notice was not properly served).

Compensation is not payable in respect of **any activity which, at the time when the notice is in force, constitutes or contributes to a breach of planning control** (s 186(5)).

If it transpires that the stop notice or the enforcement notice is a nullity, and so incapable of being withdrawn or quashed, no compensation is payable.

Compensation is payable by the local planning authority to any person who has an interest in or who occupies land to which the stop notice relates and who suffers loss which is directly attributable to complying with the relevant prohibition in the stop notice (s 186(2)). Compensation is payable for any breach of contract caused as a result of complying with the prohibition (s 186(4)).

Compensation is not payable in respect of any loss or damage which could have been avoided if the claimant had provided information required of him following requisitions for information served under sections 171C or 330 of the 1990 Act, or under section 16 of the Local Government (Miscellaneous Provisions) Act 1976 (s 186(5)).

Criminal liability for failure to comply with enforcement notice

Offences for failure to comply with an enforcement notice are created by section 179(2) and (5) of the 1990 Act. Both offences are triable either way.

1. Offence under section 179(2)

The owner of premises to which an enforcement notice relates is guilty of an offence if **at any time after the period for compliance has** expired any step required by the notice to be taken has not been taken, or any activity required to cease has not ceased (s 179(1) and (2)). The offence is committed once the time for compliance has expired.

The prosecution does not have to prove that the owner himself caused or was responsible for the breach of the enforcement notice. However, it is a defence for the owner to prove that **he did everything he could be expected to do to secure compliance with the notice** (s 179(3)). This defence will cover those situations where the owner is in no position to secure compliance with the enforcement notice (*e.g.* because the premises are let). In appropriate circumstances the defence may be established where the defendant's personal or financial circumstances mean that he genuinely cannot be expected to comply with the notice[11].

Liability under section 179(2) attaches to any subsequent owner of the land for as long as the enforcement notice is not complied with. Liability under section 179(2) is strict. There is no need for the local planning authority to prove that the defendant had knowledge of the enforcement notice[12].

2. Offence under section 179(5)

The offence under section 179(2) only applies to the owner of premises to which the enforcement notice relates. A separate offence is created by section 179(4) and (5) for a non–owner who **has control of an interest in the land to which an enforcement notice relates**. Such a person **must not carry on any activity which is required by the notice to cease or cause or permit such an activity to be carried on** (s 179(4)). This offence can only be committed after the time for compliance has expired.

This offence only applies to activities required to cease by the enforcement notice. A defendant is only guilty if he himself carried on the offending activity or caused or permitted it to be carried on. To prove that the defendant "permitted" an activity to take place the prosecution must show that the defendant had the power to prevent the activity from taking place, and that he failed to take reasonable steps so to prevent it[13].

3. Prosecution of enforcement notice offences

Charging the offence
Either offence may be charged by reference to a single day or any longer period of time. Where a defendant has been convicted of either offence

---

[11]*Kent CC v Brockman* [1994] JPL B27.
[12]*R v Collett* [1994] 1 WLR 475.
[13]*Ragsdale v Creswick* [1984] JPL 883.

he may be prosecuted for a subsequent offence if, after the date of the first conviction, he continues to be in breach of the enforcement notice (s 179(6)).

Ignorance of the enforcement notice
A narrow defence to both the offences based on ignorance of the enforcement notice is provided by section 179(7). It is a defence to either offence for the defendant to prove that **he was not aware of the existence of the notice** provided that the defendant was **not served with a copy of the enforcement notice** and **the notice is not contained in the appropriate register kept under section 188** (s 179(7)).

Section 188 provides for a register to be kept by a local planning authority of all enforcement notices, stop notices and breach of condition notices issued by it. This register has to be open to public inspection. In particular, subsequent purchasers of the land should become aware of the existence of any enforcement notices relating to the land by inspection of the register.

It follows that, provided that the enforcement notice was placed on the register, the defence is not available even though a defendant was not served with it and was not aware of it.

Challenging the validity of the enforcement notice
Subject to a narrow exception[14], on a prosecution for either offence it is not open to the defence to challenge the validity of an enforcement notice on any of the grounds that could be raised on an appeal to the Secretary of State (s 285(1)).

Criminal liability for failure to comply with stop notice

It is an offence if **any person contravenes a stop notice after a site notice has been displayed or the stop notice has been served on him** (s 187(1)). A stop notice cannot be contravened until it has taken effect (s 184(2)). A stop notice cannot take effect less than three days after service (unless there are special reasons for urgency) (s 184(3)). The offence is triable either way.

Without a site notice only persons served with the stop notice can be liable. The posting of a site notice imposes liability on all persons involved in the relevant activity.

---

[14]This prohibition does not apply to a person charged with an offence under section 179 if he has held his interest since before the issue of the enforcement notice, was not served with the enforcement notice and satisfies the court that he did not have and could not reasonably have been expected to have knowledge that the enforcement notice had been issued, and that his interests have been substantially prejudiced by the failure to serve him (s 285(2)).

Contravening a stop notice includes **causing or permitting its contravention** (s 187(1B)). The meaning of "permitting" is discussed above on page 75.

There is no equivalent of section 285 of the 1990 Act for stop notices. It is possible to challenge the validity of a stop notice by way of a defence to criminal proceedings, for example on the ground that the activities in question cannot be restrained by a stop notice[15] or are not in breach of planning control[16].

It is a defence for the defendant to prove that **the stop notice was not served on him** and **that he did not know, and could not reasonably have been expected to know, of its existence** (s 187(3)).

The offence may be charged by reference to a single day or any longer period of time. Where a defendant has been convicted he may be prosecuted for a subsequent offence if, after the date of the first conviction, he continues to be in breach of the stop notice (s 187(1A)).

[15]*R v Jenner* [1983] JPL 547.
[16]*R v Dhar* [1993] 2 PLR 60.

Breach of Condition Notices

CHAPTER 9

Breach of Condition Notices

Introduction

The Planning and Compensation Act 1991 introduced section 187A into the 1990 Act. This provided, with effect from 27 July 1992, a new method of enforcement specifically designed to deal with breach of conditions, namely **breach of condition notices**. The idea was to provide a speedy method for securing compliance with conditions which did not expose the relevant conditions to review. As a result there is no right of appeal against a breach of condition notice to the Secretary of State.

Guidance on the service of breach of condition notices is given in Annex 2 of Circular 17/92.

Outline of breach of condition notices

1. Scope

Section 187A applies where planning permission for development has been granted subject to conditions (s 187A(1)). By subsection (2):

> The local planning authority may, if any of the conditions is not complied with, serve a notice (in this Act referred to as a 'breach of condition notice') on—
>
> (a) any person who is carrying out or has carried out the development; or
> (b) any person having control of the land,
>
> requiring him to secure compliance with such of the conditions as are specified in the notice.

By section 187A(13)(b) carrying out development includes **causing or permitting another to do so**.

Unlike enforcement notices, breach of condition notices do not have to be served on all persons with an interest in the land. Indeed paragraph 13 of Annex 2 of Circular 17/92 suggests that a breach of condition notice should normally only have one recipient.

A breach of condition notice served on the person who has carried out the development (subs (2)(a)) can relate to any kind of condition, but such notice served on a person having control of the land (under subs (2)(b)) can only relate to **conditions regulating the use of land** (s 187A(4)). The assumption is that the person currently in control of land can be expected to do something about a breach of condition relating to the way in which the land is used, but not about a breach of any other kind of condition (*e.g.* one regulating how building operations are to be carried out) perpetrated by someone else.

A breach of condition notice can relate to more than one condition.

2. Requirements

The breach of condition notice must specify **the steps which the authority consider ought to be taken, or the activities which the authority consider ought to cease, to secure compliance with the conditions specified in the notice** (s 187A(5)).

3. Period for compliance

A breach of condition notice must specify the period within which it has to be complied with. Section 187A(7) provides that this period shall be:

(a) such period of not less than twenty-eight days beginning with the date of service of the notice as may be specified in the notice; or
(b) that period as extended by a further notice served by the local planning authority on the person responsible.

4. Form

There is no set form for a breach of condition notice. However a model notice is set out in the Appendix to Annex 2 of Circular 17/92.

5. Limitations

Subsection (13)(a) provides that for the purposes of section 187A **"conditions" includes limitations**. The term "limitations" is not an easy one to interpret; it is not defined in the Act. Paragraph 5 of Annex 2 of Circular 17/92 states that "the reference to conditions includes reference to limitations which are statutorily imposed by certain of the provisions for 'permitted development' rights in [the General Permitted Development Order]".

Some permitted development rights have clear limitations (*e.g.* the 28-day time limit on certain temporary permissions). However, in some instances restrictions in the scope of General Permitted Development Order permissions are imposed by the identification of "development not permitted" (*e.g.* size limits on house roof extensions under Class B of Part 1). It is unclear whether breach of these restrictions could be enforced by breach of condition notice.

6. No appeal to Secretary of State
There is no right of appeal to the Secretary of State against a breach of condition notice. As a result, the service of such notice does not give the recipient the opportunity to seek a review of the planning merits of the relevant condition. As a result there is no equivalent to section 285 of the 1990 Act (see Chap 8) for breach of condition notices.

7. Register
The local planning authority must enter all breach of condition notices that it issues on the register kept (s 188 of the 1990 Act).

8. Withdrawal
By subsection (6) the local planning authority

> may by notice served on the person responsible withdraw the breach of condition notice, but its withdrawal shall not affect the power to serve on him a further breach of condition notice in respect of the conditions specified in the earlier notice or any other conditions.

The local planning authority can withdraw a breach of condition notice at any time, including after the period for compliance has expired.

Criminal liability

1. Offence under section 187A(9)
Section 187A(8) and (9) provide as follows:

> (8) If, at any time after the period allowed for compliance with the notice—
>
> (a) any of the conditions specified in the notice is not complied with; and
> (b) the steps specified in the notice have not been taken or, as the case may be, the activities specified in the notice have not ceased,
>
> the person responsible is in breach of the notice.
>
> (9) If the person responsible is in breach of the notice he shall be guilty of an offence.

By subsection (3) **references in this section to the person responsible are to the person on whom the breach of condition notice has been served**.

The criminal offence is committed by the person on whom the notice has been served if the condition is not complied with *and* the requirements of the notice are not met within the time identified. It is important to note the two elements to the offence. Thus, if the condition is complied with within the relevant time, albeit without actually carrying out the steps identified in the notice, no offence is committed.

2. Defence under subsection (11)(a)

It is a defence under subsection (11)(a) for the defendant to prove **that he took all reasonable measures to secure compliance with the conditions specified in the notice**. Reasonable measures to secure compliance with the conditions may not be the same as the steps identified in the breach of condition notice. Indeed, if the steps identified in the notice are unduly harsh it may be open to the defendant to argue that it was reasonable for him to carry out other lesser measures.

This defence is similar to the defence under section 179(3) for failure to comply with an enforcement notice (namely that the defendant did everything he could be expected to do to secure compliance with the notice). This defence is discussed in Chapter 8.

3. Defence under subsection (11)(b)

The second defence under subsection (11) only applies where a breach of condition notice has been served under subsection (2)(b) (ie on the basis that the defendant has control of the land). It is a defence under subsection (11)(b) for such person to show that **he no longer had control of the land**.

The burden of proving either of the statutory defences lies on the defendant.

4. Defence based on challenge to condition/breach of condition notice

The availability of defences based on challenging the validity of the breach of condition notice, or the condition on which it is based, is not straightforward. It is determined by the operation of two factors. On the one hand, as has been pointed out above, there is no statutory restriction (like section 285 for enforcement notices) to the making of challenges to the validity of the breach of condition notice. On the other hand, it is now established that the invalidity of an act or decision of a public body cannot be raised as a defence to a prosecution unless the act or decision is invalid on its face. This principle emerges from two recent decisions, *Bugg* v *DPP* [1993] QB 473 (a decision concerning a prosecution under bylaws made under the Military Lands Act 1892) and *R* v *Wicks, The Times*, 19 April 1995 (a decision concerning a prosecution for breach of an enforcement notice). In *Wicks* the Court of Appeal held that the invalidity of an enforcement notice could only be raised by way of a defence if the notice was invalid on its face, and so a nullity. Any other challenge to the validity of the notice could only be raised by way of judicial review. If a prosecution was in progress the appropriate course would be to adjourn the criminal proceedings to allow the judicial review to be pursued.

The general law relating to judicial review and the validity of the decisions of public bodies is beyond the scope of this work. However, three points can be made.

First, the absence of any right of appeal to the Secretary of State against a breach of condition notice must mean that it would be open to a defendant in criminal proceedings to raise by way of defence an allegation that the breach of condition is immune from enforcement action by reason of effluxion of time, or that the matters alleged do not amount to a breach of the relevant condition.

Secondly, there may be instances where failure to comply with one of the legal requirements mentioned in Chapter 2 renders a condition invalid on its face. For example a condition might bear no relation to the development permitted, or require the payment of money, or impose a positive requirement on land outside the application site and outside the applicant's control. A defence based on the nullity of such a condition would fall within the principle in *Wicks*. Similarly the breach of condition notice itself may be invalid on its face if its terms do not comply with the requirements of section 187A. Paragraph 20 of Annex 2 of Circular 17/92 advises that, where there is doubt about the legality of a condition, a breach of condition notice may be inappropriate, and an enforcement notice should be used instead.

Thirdly, failure to comply with the requirements of section 187A itself may provide the basis for a defence—for example, if the defendant is not someone who could be served with a breach of condition notice under the section.

5. Charging the offence

Subsection (10) provides that the offence under subsection (9)

> may be charged by reference to any day or longer period of time and a person may be convicted of a second or subsequent offence under that subsection by reference to any period of time following the preceding conviction for such an offence.

6. Summary offence

The offence is a summary offence, punishable only with a fine not exceeding level 3 on the standard scale (s 187A(12)). Being a summary offence any prosecution must be started within six months of the commission of the offence. The offence under subsection (9) is a continuing offence. It starts to be committed when the time for compliance has expired, and continues for as long as the relevant requirements are not fulfilled. A prosecution can relate to as much of the period of non–compliance as occurred within the six months prior to the launch of proceedings. It does not matter that the first date of non–compliance is outside the six-month period.

Effect of subsequent grant of planning permission

It may happen that, during the course of proceedings for failure to comply with a breach of condition notice, an application for planning permission to permit the offending development is being considered. Such an application could take the form of an application for variation of the offending condition under section 73 (see Chap 6), or an application for planning permission to retain the development without complying with the condition (under s 73A(2)(c)). In a situation where the local planning authority regards a breach of condition notice as appropriate it is unlikely that such an application would be granted by them, with the result that such an application may only finally be determined by an appeal to the Secretary of State.

The effect of the grant of permission/discharge of condition on a breach of condition notice is governed by section 180 (discussed in Chap 8 at page 70). The breach of condition notice ceases to have effect to the extent that it is inconsistent with the grant of permission/discharge of condition (s 180(1) and (2)). Any criminal liability that arises as a result of events before the grant/discharge is preserved (s 180(3)).

Government Policy and Particular Conditions

CHAPTER 10

Government Policy and Particular Conditions

Guidance on the imposition of conditions generally, and on certain particular conditions, is given in Circular 11/95 which is set out in full in Appendix 1. The Circular does not regulate the legal status of conditions (their validity or invalidity)[1], but indicates when, in planning terms, they will be acceptable. A local planning authority should not impose a condition that breaches the guidance: if it does, the Secretary of State will discharge the condition on appeal.

Unless otherwise indicated, all references to paragraphs in this chapter are to paragraphs in the Annex to Circular 11/95.

Requirements of Circular 11/95

The Circular lays down six tests that all conditions must comply with. These reflect, and, to an extent, supplement the legal test for the validity of conditions discussed in Chapter 2.

1. Necessary
Local planning authorities should ask themselves whether "planning permission would have to be refused if [a] condition were not to be imposed". If not, the condition needs "special and precise justification" (para 15). A condition may be considered unnecessary if it would not be expedient to take enforcement action in the event of a breach (para 16). A condition should not be wider in scope than is necessary (para 17). There is no legal requirement that conditions should be necessary in this sense.

A condition may be unnecessary if a particular matter is regulated by a planning obligation.

[1] *Ashford BC* v *Secretary of State for the Environment and Hume* [1992] JPL 363 is authority for the proposition that the mere fact that a condition does not satisfy the six tests set out in the Circular does not make the condition invalid.

A condition will be unnecessary if it seeks to prevent an activity that would in any event require planning permission[2].

2. Relevant to planning

A condition must achieve a purpose that is relevant to planning (paras 20–23). This test reflects the legal requirement discussed in Chapter 2. One aspect of this requirement is that if a particular aspect of a proposed development is subject to specific control by other planning legislation (*e.g.* advertisement control), the local planning authority should rely on that other legislation and not attempt to police the matter by imposing a condition (para 21). Some matters relevant to planning are controlled by other legislation entirely (*e.g.* licensing). In these cases, again conditions should not be imposed unless, under paragraph 23,

> "the considerations material to the exercise of the two systems of control are substantially different, since it might be unwise in these circumstances to rely on the alternative control being exercised in the manner or to the degree needed to secure planning objectives. Conditions may also be needed to deal with circumstances for which a concurrent control is unavailable ... [or] where they can prevent development being carried out in a manner which would be likely to give rise to onerous requirements under other powers at a later stage (*e.g.* to ensure adequate sewerage and water supply for new development and thus avoid subsequent intervention under the Public Health Acts)."

3. Relevant to the development permitted

A condition must be relevant to the development permitted by the grant of planning permission (paras 24–5). This test again reflects the legal requirement discussed in Chapter 2. A condition must be called for by the nature of the development permitted. In some instances this may justify the regulation of existing facilities if they will be affected by the proposed development.

4. Enforceable

A condition should not be imposed if it cannot be enforced (paras 26–9). A condition may be unenforceable if it would be impractical to monitor (para 27). This test goes beyond the legal requirements—practical difficulties in enforcement do not constitute a separate head of legal challenge[3].

---

[2]See *Westminster City Council* v *Dukegrade Ltd* [1990] JPL 277 and *Westminster City Council* v *Miller Developments Ltd* [1992] JPL 24 where conditions sought to prevent use of residential premises for use as temporary sleeping accommodation, a use that would have required planning permission in any event.
[3]*Bromsgrove DC* v *Secretary of State for the Environment* [1988] JPL 257.

5. Precise

A condition must be precise (paras 30–33). The test laid down in the Circular goes beyond the legal requirements for certainty discussed in Chapter 2. Conditions should be worded so as to achieve their objectives effectually. Thus, as the Circular points out, a landscaping condition should not only require that a landscaping scheme should be submitted for the approval of the local planning authority: it should also require that the scheme is carried out at a particular stage in the development.

Vague terms in conditions, and terms that do not provide objective and certain criteria to enable the developer to assess what he is required to do, must be avoided (para 31). Such conditions would probably be ultra vires.

An imprecise or unreasonable condition cannot be made acceptable by making the local planning authority the arbiter (*e.g.* by requiring that something imprecise should be done "to the satisfaction of the local planning authority" or that something imprecise should not be done "except with the prior approval of the local planning authority") (para 32).

6. Reasonable

A condition must be reasonable (paras 34–42). This test mirrors the legal test. In addition, conditions which are not ultra vires should not be imposed if they are unduly onerous—*e.g.* conditions which make it difficult for an owner to dispose of his property, or which would make the development difficult to finance (para 36).

It is possible, in principle, to have a condition which requires a developer to carry out works on land within the application site but not within his control. However, it may not be reasonable to enforce such a condition. This problem can often be avoided by using an appropriate *Grampian* condition (paras 37 and 28). Similarly, it is unreasonable to impose a positive condition which a developer cannot comply with without the consent or authorisation of a third party. Again an appropriate *Grampian* condition may overcome this problem (paras 38–9).

It is the Secretary of State's policy that a *Grampian* condition should only be imposed if there is a reasonable prospect of the relevant action being performed during the period for implementation of the permission (para 40). (A similar point is made in paragraph 3 of Annex C of PPG 13, dealing with the imposition of negative conditions depending on the carrying out of highway works.) As has been seen in Chapter 2, there is no legal requirement that there should be a reasonable prospect of the occurrence of the event on which a *Grampian* condition is contingent.

An unreasonable condition does not become reasonable just because the developer consents to its terms (Annex, para 35).

Particular conditions

The Circular gives detailed guidance on the imposition and wording of conditions in a number of circumstances. It also gives, in Appendix A, a list of 79 model conditions and, in Appendix B, a list of 13 unacceptable conditions.

The Circular is obviously the principal source of guidance on the form and wording of conditions in particular instances. There follows below a discussion of some of the points made in the Circular, and of other points made in decisions of inspectors, of the Secretary of State and of the courts.

There is no obligation on an inspector to cast around to find conditions to make a development acceptable (*Top Deck Holdings Ltd* v *Secretary of State for the Environment* [1991] JPL 961).

1. General points

Condition unrelated to development

Examples of invalid conditions

Condition in planning permission for extension to stables requiring painting of existing roof (appeal decision reported at [1983] JPL 762).

Condition restricting opening hours of café in planning permission for use of gaming machines in café which previously had unrestricted opening hours (appeal decision reported at [1985] JPL 507).

Condition relating to buildings not within the bounds of planning permission (appeal decision reported at [1984] JPL 199).

Example of valid condition

Agricultural occupancy condition on existing house in planning permission for second house (acceptable because construction of second house created possibility that first house might cease to be used as a farmhouse) (appeal decision reported at [1982] JPL 208). See similar decision reported at [1992] JPL 191.

Matters covered by other legislation

> *Examples of inappropriate conditions*
>
> Condition covering construction of building and its drainage (unnecessary as matters dealt with by building regulations) (appeal decision reported at [1966]] JPL 290).
>
> Condition restricting display of advertisements (unnecessary as control provided by advertisement regulations) (appeal decision reported at [1971] JPL 716).
>
> Condition on industrial plant controlling noise and fumes (unnecessary as conditions duplicated controls in the Alkali and Clean Air Acts) (appeal decision reported at [1977] JPL 820).

Matters already subject to planning cotrol
When development is permitted it is unnecessary to impose a condition to prevent a particular operation or change of use from taking place subsequently if such change would require planning permission in any event.

> *Example*
>
> Condition imposed on planning permission for new houses in Westminster preventing change of use to temporary sleeping accommodation within the meaning of the Greater London (General Powers) Act 1973 unnecessary because a change from residential use to use for temporary sleeping accommodation would require planning permission in any event (*Westminster City Council* v *Dukegrade Ltd* [1990] JPL 277 and *Westminster City Council* v *Miller Developments Ltd* [1992] JPL 24).

Removal of permitted development/established use rights
Conditions can prevent the carrying out of activities that would not otherwise require planning permission (by reason not being development at all, or by reason of the operation of the Use Classes Order, or the General Permitted Development Order).

There is a general presumption against conditions which remove rights conferred by the General Permitted Development Order or the Use Classes Order. Any such condition should be no more onerous than necessary. The activity or use sought prevented by such a condition should be identified as precisely as possible (paras 86–90; model conditions 48, 50–52).

Conditions preventing ancillary uses should not normally be imposed on manufacturing or service industry except where designed to preclude or regulate activities giving rise to hazards, noise or offensive emissions (para 91).

Examples of invalid conditions

Planning permission for retention of a building cannot contain a condition seeking to remove existing use rights (appeal decision reported at [1970] JPL 542).

Condition taking away permitted development rights in permission for approval of reserved matters following grant of outline planning permission (appeal decision reported at [1967] JPL 726).

Detracting from existing planning permission
A condition in one planning permission can detract from the rights conferred by another, earlier planning permission (*Peak Park Joint Planning Board* v *Secretary of State for the Environment* [1980] JPL 114).

Conditions altering the nature of the development
See paragraph 84.

Outline planning permission and reserved matters
Conditions relating to any matters other than the reserved matters themselves (for example restrictions on the development that are applicable whatever precise form it may take) must be imposed in the original grant of outline permission (para 45).

An approval of reserved matters can be subject to conditions, but the conditions must relate only to the reserved matters (para 45; appeal decision reported at [1990] JPL 863; and *R* v *Elmbridge BC ex p Health Care Corp Ltd* [1992] JPL 39).

In appropriate cases, matters in full permissions and matters other than reserved matters in outline permissions can be required to be submitted to the local planning authority for its approval before development is begun (*e.g.* car parking spaces) (para 47). A planning permission for a change of use (tipping) can contain conditions requiring certain matters to be approved later (materials to be tipped) (*Roberts* v *Vale Royal DC* (1977) 39 P&CR 514).

It is possible to seek and receive a number of different approvals of the same reserved matter (para 57). A reserved matters conditions should not require approval to be obtained within a specific time (para 58).

For appropriate form of reserved matters conditions in outline permissions, see model conditions 2–5.

2. Conditions relating to the timing of development

Timing of development
Conditions can, in appropriate circumstances, require development to be phased (para 63; model condition 42).

A condition in a planning permission for a complex of development requiring whole development to be started simultaneously and completed as a whole was held to be invalid in an appeal decision reported at [1979] JPL 549.

Implementation
The law on the implementation of planning permissions is discussed in Chapter 5. (See paras 53–9; model conditions 1–5.)

Completion of development
Conditions requiring that a specific aspect of a development should be provided are preferable to conditions requiring the entire development should be completed. A condition requiring the entire development to be completed is often unnecessary (paras 18, 61–2).

3. Personal and temporary conditions

Personal conditions
These are normally only justified where a development would not ordinarily be acceptable, but there are compassionate or other personal reasons for allowing a particular individual to carry them out (para 93; model conditions 35–6).

Examples

A personal condition is scarcely ever justified in a planning permission for permanent development (appeal decision reported at [1992] JPL 391).

A condition in a planning permission for the construction of a new house requiring that permission be implemented by the applicant failed to meet any of the six tests in Circular 11/95, and was held to be unreasonable (appeal decision reported at [1992] JPL 284).

A personal planning permission was acceptable where this was necessary to prevent an intensification of use (appeal decision reported at [1989] JPL 462).

Temporary permission

It is normally inappropriate to grant temporary permission for development intended to be permanent. Temporary permissions will normally only be appropriate where this is all the applicant seeks, or where a trial run is needed. Temporary permissions may also be appropriate where a building or use is only expected to be short term (for example because the land will be taken for highway works) (paras 108–13; model condition 41).

The reason for a temporary permission can never be the effect of the development on the amenities of the area (para 109; appeal decisions reported at [1981] JPL 695 and [1985] JPL 70).

Seasonal use

See paragraphs 115–7.

4. Occupancy conditions

The identity of an occupier is normally irrelevant for planning purposes. Conditions restricting occupation of a development to a particular occupier or class of occupiers should therefore only be used where special grounds exist, and where the alternative would be refusal of the application (para 92).

Commercial development

In exceptional circumstances (where the need of a local firm to expand justifies granting permission for development in breach of restraint policies) it may be appropriate to limit occupation of commercial premises to local firms, provided that the restriction is for a limited period and the catchment area is sufficiently large. Those who may occupy the premises should be specified (para 95; model condition 44).

Conditions requiring an industrial unit to be occupied either as a single unit or in units of particular sizes should normally be avoided (para 106).

> *Examples*
>
> The Secretary of State requires good reason to justify the imposition of a local occupancy condition. A condition limiting occupation of industrial premises to businesses with two years' occupation in areas specified in a local plan was upheld (*Slough Industrial Estates* v *Secretary of State for the Environment* [1987] JPL 353).
>
> Conditions which gave a local planning authority discretion to vet acceptable occupiers for commercial premises are

unacceptable (appeal decisions reported at [1977] JPL 398 and [1980] JPL 212).

A condition limiting the length of stay of residents imposed in a hostel planning permission was held to be reasonable in *Commercial and Residential Property Development Co Ltd* v *Secretary of State for the Environment* (1982) 80 LGR 443.

Domestic occupancy conditions (non-agricultural)
Subject to guidance about affordable housing, staff accommodation, agricultural dwellings and seasonal uses, there is "seldom any good reason" to impose conditions restricting the occupation of residential premises to certain categories of person (para 96).

Examples

A condition restricting occupation of a dwelling to a gipsy or a dependent residing with a gipsy or the widow/widower of such a person was upheld in an appeal decision reported at [1992] JPL 510.

In an appeal decision reported at [1992] JPL 1093 it was held that a restriction designed to ensure that sheltered housing would only be occupied by the elderly could not be achieved by condition. It could only be achieved by a planning obligation.

Low cost housing
There may be circumstances where it is acceptable to restrict some housing in a development to occupation by persons falling within particular categories of need (para 97).

An appeal decision reported at [1994] JPL 1 gives the form of a condition (based on a DoE draft consultation paper of December 1992) to be used to ensure that residential development functions as low cost housing.

Agricultural occupancy conditions
Residential development may sometimes be allowed in countryside areas where it is necessary to provide accommodation for a farmworker near to the farm. In such cases a condition limiting the occupation of the premises to someone engaged in agriculture may be appropriate (paras 102–5; model condition 45). More specific guidance is given in PPG 7, Annex E.

Agricultural occupancy conditions and the considerations relevant to their imposition were discussed in *Kember v Secretary of State for the Environment and Tunbridge Wells BC* [1982] JPL 383 and *Peak Park Joint Planning Board v Secretary of State for the Environment* [1980] JPL 114. See *Millbank v Secretary of State for the Environment and Rochford DC* (1991) 61 P&CR 11 for observations on the approach to be taken to the discharge of such conditions.

Staff accommodation and granny annexes
See paragraphs 98–101 and model condition 47.

5. Specific conditions

Housing mix
Exceptional circumstances are required to justify the imposing of a condition regulating the size of houses to be built in an outline planning permission (appeal decision reported at [1988] JPL 509). It was held to be legitimate to impose a condition requiring 25% of units to be provided to mobility standards in an appeal decision reported at [1992] JPL 403.

Access
A condition can require that all access to a development should be by means of a given service road, and can require works to such a road (even though it is not in the application), provided that it is either within the application site or within the developer's control. Such a condition should be negatively worded. A condition cannot require cession of land to a highway authority (paras 69–70, 72; model conditions 14–19).

Conditions requiring demolition
A condition requiring the demolition of existing buildings is rarely likely to be acceptable in a planning permission concerned only with the use of the buildings (*Newbury DC v Secretary of State for the Environment* [1981] AC 578).

Examples

A condition in a planning permission for an extension requiring the demolition of the extension and the existing building after a period of time was unreasonable (appeal decision reported at [1967] JPL 239).

A condition in a planning permission for a chalet that was intended to be permanent requiring demolition after 10 years was unreasonable (appeal decision reported at [1987] JPL 147).

Payment of money
A condition cannot require the payment of money (para 83).

Conditions requiring development to be carried out according to the application
A local planning authority can take enforcement action against development that is materially different from the approved design. However, it may be easier to take action against a breach of condition. It may therefore be appropriate to incorporate important features of the application into a condition (*e.g.* hours of operation) (para 19; model condition 79).

Other matters

- Landscaping and trees (paras 48–52; model conditions 25–32).
- Car parking (paras 64–8; model conditions 20–2)
- Maintenance conditions (para 82)
- Access for the disabled (para 114; model condition 37)
- Drainage (model conditions 38–40)
- Hours of use (model conditions 65–8)
- Amenity land (model conditions 76–8)
- Retail development (para 107; model condition 49)

6. Matters dealt with in other Circulars/PPGs
Guidance on conditions appropriate to certain other circumstances is dealt with in other PPGs and Circulars. The references are as follows:

- Protection of trees on development sites (Circular 36/78, para 75 (and Circular 11/95, model conditions 71–5))
- Reuse of redundant agricultural buildings in the Green Belt (PPG 2, para 16. This paragraph was said to create an exception to *Top Deck Holdings Ltd* v *Secretary of State for the Environment* [1991] JPL 961 in *Murphy* v *Secretary of State for Wales and Torfaen BC* [1994] JPL 156)
- Industrial development (PPG 4, paras 27–31)
- Agricultural occupancy conditions (PPG 7, Annex E (and Circular 11/95, paras 102–5 and model condition 45))
- Nature conservation (PPG 9, para 28 (and Circular 11/95 paras 118–120))
- Works in the highway (PPG 13, Annex C)
- Development on unstable land (PPG 14, paras 36–45)
- Development on archaeological sites (PPG 16, paras 29–30 (and Circular 11/95, paras 80–81 and model conditions 53–5))
- Pollution control (PPG 23, paras 3.23–8 (and Circular 11/95, para 77))

- Contaminated land (PPG 23, Annex 10, paras 8–11 (and Circular 11/95, paras 73–6 and model conditions 56–9, and appeal decision reported at [1995] JPL 763))
- Restoration of landfill sites (PPG 23, Annex 11, paras 1–5)
- Noise (PPG 24, paras 15–9 (and Circular 11/95, para 28 and model conditions 6–11))

7. Miscellaneous unreasonable conditions

The following are examples of other conditions that have been found to be unreasonable.

Condition restricting the use of car parking space to residents of a particular London Borough (appeal decision reported at [1991] JPL 184).

Condition requiring developer to satisfy the local planning authority of the existence of a right of way (appeal decision reported at [1968] JPL 306).

Condition requiring a developer to enter into an agreement under section 52 of the Town and Country Planning Act 1971 (appeal decision reported at [1980] JPL 841).

Condition requiring that plant and machinery should be removed "at such time as the local planning authority is satisfied, after consultation with the developers, that this is no longer needed" was invalid because it made the local planning authority the arbiter of the time at which the machinery should be removed. The fact that the condition made provision for consultation with the developer made no difference to this (appeal decision reported at [1994] JPL 476).

Condition requiring vehicles visiting a site to use certain routes (*Mouchell Superannuation Trustees* v *Oxfordshire CC* [1992] 1 PLR 97).

PART II

Planning Obligations

CHAPTER II

Planning Obligations—Scope and Legal Requirements

CHAPTER 11

Planning Obligations—Scope and Legal Requirements

Introduction

Some restrictions on development and some undertakings to do works cannot be achieved by condition. In such a situation a developer will only be able to commit himself to such measures, if at all, by entering into a planning obligation under section 106 of the 1990 Act. The present version of section 106 was inserted into the Act in 1991 and created a new way by which landowners could create obligations affecting their land. In summary, a planning obligation is a formal undertaking created by a deed which binds the land of the party entering into it, and is enforceable by the local planning authority. A landowner can create a planning obligation unilaterally or by agreement with the local planning authority. The restrictions on planning obligations and the requirements for creating them are discussed in detail below.

An important use of planning obligation is to secure contributions to the costs of off–site infrastructure works required in association with development from developers[1].

Scope of planning obligations

Section 106(1) defines the scope of planning obligations. It provides:

> Any person interested in land in the area of a local planning authority may, by agreement or otherwise, enter into an obligation (referred to in this section and sections 106A and 106B as 'a planning obligation') enforceable to the extent mentioned in subsection (3)—
>
> (a) restricting the development or use of the land in any specified way;
> (b) requiring specific operations or activities to be carried out in, on, under or over the land;

[1] In this connection it should be noted that there is also a wide power under section 278 of the Highways Act 1980 to enter into agreements to contribute to the cost of highway works.

(c) requiring the land to be used in any specified way; or

(d) requiring a sum or sums to be paid to the authority on a specified date or dates or periodically.

Test of validity

A number of recent cases have considered the fundamental requirements of planning obligations. In *Good* v *Epping Forest DC* [1994] JPL 373 the Court of Appeal had occasion to consider the circumstances in which an agreement made under section 52 of the Town and Country Planning Act 1971, the predecessor to section 106, might be invalid, and so not binding on the relevant landowner. *R* v *South Northamptonshire DC ex p Crest Homes plc* [1995] JPL 200 and *Tesco Stores Ltd* v *Secretary of State for the Environment* [1995] JPL 581 indicate that the reasoning in *Good* also applies to planning obligations.

The following points emerge from these decisions.

1. Must be made for a planning purpose

The Court of Appeal in *Good* held that a section 52 agreement would only be valid if it was made for a planning purpose, the first test in *Newbury DC* v *Secretary of State for the Environment* [1981] AC 578. This test also applies to planning obligations[2].

The reasoning in *Good* was based on the wording of section 52. This said that such agreements had to be made **for the purposes of restricting or regulating the use or development of land**. Similar words appear in section 106(1)(a)–(c), so that planning obligations under those provisions will, by definition, relate to planning. The wording of subsection (d) (**requiring a sum or sums to be paid to the authority on a specified date or dates or periodically**) is apparently wider. However, a local planning authority would not be entitled to receive payments of money that were not made for a planning purpose.

2. Must be reasonable

A planning obligation must not be unreasonable (the third requirement in *Newbury*). It makes no difference to this that the planning obligation is created by agreement. A local planning authority would presumably not be able to enforce an unreasonable planning obligation that had been created unilaterally.

[2]*R* v *South Northamptonshire DC ex p Crest Homes plc* [1995] JPL 200 at p 212 and *Tesco Stores Ltd* v *Secretary of State for the Environment* [1995] JPL 581 at p 597.

The test of unreasonableness in a planning obligation will, in some instances, differ from the test of unreasonableness in a condition[3]. As is made clear below, there are types of obligations that can be imposed by planning obligation which cannot be imposed by condition. The mere fact that a restriction would be unreasonable if imposed by a condition does not mean that it will be unreasonable if contained in a planning obligation.

3. No requirement of fair and reasonable relationship to development

There is no requirement that planning obligations should fairly and reasonably relate to the development (the second test in *Newbury*). Indeed, as is pointed out below, there is no requirement that a planning obligation should accompany a proposal for development at all.

For this reason planning obligations will be able to achieve restrictions that cannot be achieved by the imposition of conditions.

Other legal parameters

Apart from the points considered above, the scope of what can be achieved by means of a planning obligation is determined by the terms of section 106 itself. The relevant provisions are considered below.

It is important to stress at the outset that there is no requirement that any development requiring planning permission should be intended before a planning obligation can be created. However, most planning obligations will in fact accompany the grant of planning permission.

1. "... by agreement or otherwise ..." (s 106(1))

Planning obligations can be created **by agreement or otherwise** (s 106(1)). This is an extremely important provision. It means that a landowner can create a planning obligation unilaterally. The result will still be a legally binding obligation, enforceable by the local planning authority. Previously legally binding obligations could only be created by agreement. This often produced problems on appeal. If a development could only be made acceptable by the developer subjecting himself to a legal obligation covering a matter that could not be dealt with by condition (*e.g.* the funding of off-site infrastructure works), the local planning authority could frustrate the creation of the obligation by refusing to agree to it.

[3]*Tesco Stores Ltd* v *Secretary of State for the Environment* [1995] JPL 581 at p 597.

2. "... person interested in land ..." (s 106(1))

As discussed in Chapter 13, planning obligations bind land, and will, in appropriate circumstances, be enforceable against land. A person entering into a planning obligation must be **interested in** the land affected by the obligation (s 106(1)).

A person with no legal rights against the land in question will therefore not be able to enter into a planning obligation affecting that land. However there is authority to suggest that an interest in the strict conveyancing sense is not required.

> *Authorities*
>
> In *Jones* v *Secretary of State for Wales* (1976) 28 P&CR 280 it was held that a person who proposes to develop land, but who does not actually own an interest in it, could not enter into an agreement under section 52 of the 1971 Act (which also required that the person making the agreement should be "interested in land").
>
> But contrast *Pennine Raceways* v *Kirklees MBC* [1983] QB 382. The Court of Appeal held that a company which had a contractual licence to use land for motor racing purposes was "interested in land" for the purposes of a provision dealing with compensation following the revocation of planning permission for the motor racing use. The court expressed the view (obiter) that its reasoning would also apply to the phrase "interested in land" in section 52, and that an interest in the strict conveyancing sense was not required. This approach differs from that in *Jones*. If it were to be applied to planning obligations, a contractual licensee could enter into an obligation, although, as the licensee holds no proprietary interest in the land, the obligation would be only personal.

The interest can be of a limited nature, for example an option to purchase. As discussed in Chapter 13, it is that interest, such as it is, which is bound by the obligation. Obviously an obligation which bound only a limited interest of this kind would be of very limited value to a local planning authority.

3. "... the land ..." (s 106(1)(a)–(c))

Obligations restricting development or requiring specific operations or uses, etc (s 106(1)(a)–(c)) must impose such restrictions or requirements on "the land", that is the land in which the person creating the obligation has an interest.

An undertaking to pay money under section 106(1)(d) is not related to any land. It follows that developers can undertake to make payments for the provision of infrastructure works on land in which they have no interest. However, the person giving the undertaking must still have an interest in some land in the area of the relevant local planning authority.

The land in which the person entering into the planning obligation is interested has to be identified in the deed creating the planning obligation (s 106(9)).

4. "... specified ..." (s 106(1)(a)–(d))

Each subparagraph in section 106(1) refers to matters being "specific" or "specified". Subsection (13) provides that **in this section "specified" means specified in the instrument by which the planning obligation is entered into** ....

It seems that the specification can be by means of a document not in existence at the time of the deed, provided the document is referred to in the deed. In *South Oxfordshire DC v Secretary of State for the Environment and Eyston* [1995] JPL 213 a unilateral planning obligation provided that revenue from a golf course development should be applied for the purpose of carrying out repairs to certain listed buildings. Clause 4 of the planning obligation stated that, at the beginning of each of the next 20 years, the landowner would furnish the local planning authority with a schedule of the repairs that would be carried out in that year, such repairs being "broadly in accordance with a proof of evidence of Mr Mervyn Cable of Messrs Savills dated October 1993". It was held that the deed constituted a valid planning obligation under section 106(1)(b), in that it provided for "specific operations or activities" to be carried out with respect to the listed buildings. It was said at p 220 that "those specified operations would be identified for the purposes of subsection (13) by the operation of clause 4 ...".

5. Certainty and enforceability

There will undoubtedly be planning obligations that are invalid because they are so uncertain as to be unenforceable. However, as with conditions, the Courts are reluctant to strike down planning obligations on this ground.

Examples

South Oxfordshire DC v Secretary of State for the Environment and Eyston (above): It was held that it was open to the inspector to conclude, as a question of fact and judgment, that the planning obligation would achieve its object even though it was dependent on the landowners using "best endeavours" to let the golf course land, and on the landowners thereby obtaining sufficient funds to fund the repair works.

R v Thurrock BC ex p Tesco et al [1994] JPL 328: A planning obligation was made by the operators of a retail warehouse club. It provided that the warehouse would be operated in accordance with the operators' booklet and that goods would only be sold to club members. The booklet stated that members of the club had to belong to certain employment groups, and that groups could be altered by the operators. It was held that the planning obligation was enforceable, notwithstanding the enormous degree of discretion left to the operators, particularly with regard to defining employment groups.

6. Formalities and publicity

Section 106(9) lays down certain formal requirements for the creation of planning obligations. A planning obligation can only be created by a deed. The deed must state that the obligation is a planning obligation within section 106; must identify the person entering into the obligation, the land in which he is interested and the nature of his interest; and the local planning authority must be able to enforce the obligation.

A copy of the deed must be given to the local planning authority concerned (s 106(10)).

A planning obligation is a local land charge (s 106(11)). This means that, for the planning obligation to be enforceable against successors in title of the original landowner, it must be entered on the Local Land Charges Register. The Land Charges Register is open to public inspection. Entry on the Register is the only legal requirement for publicising a planning obligation. However, paragraph B14 of Circular 16/91 advises that local planning authorities should assist members of the public in locating planning obligations of interest to them, and that planning obligations should be listed as background papers to committee reports dealing with development proposals. Local planning authorities are told that they will need a strong case before they are justified in excluding the public from meetings discussing planning obligations.

Types of planning obligation

1. Conditional and indefinite obligations (s 106(2))
Section 106(2) provides that a planning obligation may:

(a) be unconditional or subject to conditions;

(b) impose any restriction or requirement mentioned in subsection (1)(a) to (c) either indefinitely or for such period or periods as may be specified, and

(c) if it requires a sum or sums to be paid, require the payment of a specified amount or an amount to be determined in accordance with the instrument by which the obligation is entered into and, if it requires the payment of periodical sums, require them to be paid indefinitely or for a specified period.

It follows from section 106(2)(a) that all the obligations undertaken by a developer in a planning obligation can be made conditional on the grant of planning permission for a specified development. This point has considerable practical importance. It means that a developer can complete all the formalities for the creation of a planning obligation intended to accompany a particular planning permission before the permission is granted. This is particularly convenient at an appeal. A developer can present to the inspector an executed deed which will create enforceable obligations if, and only if, his appeal is allowed and the planning permission granted is implemented.

2. Negative obligations
A planning obligation can contain a negative provision preventing development of the relevant land from taking place until some event has occurred. Such a provision operates in the same way as a *Grampian* condition and has the effect of **restricting the development or use of land** within the meaning of section 106(1)(a). Thus, in *R* v *Canterbury City Council ex p Springimage* [1994] JPL 427 a planning obligation that prohibited development of land from starting until proper sewerage arrangements were made was held to be valid even though section 106 does not cover the requisitioning of sewers.

3. Positive obligations
Planning obligations can be positive in form. They will be enforceable against future owners of the relevant interest. This represents a departure from the ordinary law of real property under which future owners can only be obliged to comply with negative obligations imposed on their land (under the rule in *Tulk* v *Moxhay*).

4. Transfers of land

Transfers of land often form part of packages of benefits offered by developers. Typically land owned by the developer and intended for use for car parking or public open space is transferred to the local planning authority. Doubt as to whether a planning obligation could be used to achieve such a transfer arose because section 106(1), though wide in its terms, makes no specific provision for transfers of land. However, the decision in *R v South Northamptonshire DC ex p Crest Homes plc* establishes that, in appropriate circumstances, a transfer of land provided for in a planning obligation can be brought within the terms of section 106(1)(a) and (c).

Transfers within section 106(1)(a) and (c)

Crest Homes holds that a planning obligation that provides for a transfer of land and also contains a *Grampian*–style restriction preventing any development on another site from taking place can be regarded as restricting the development or use of the development site within section 106(1)(a).

In addition, a planning obligation which makes provision for the way in which the land transferred is to be used falls within section 106(1)(c). One of the agreements in *Crest Homes* provided for transferred land to be leased to trustees "in order to make suitable provision for public open space within the development and to provide suitable amenities for future occupiers of the development". It thus restricted the way that the transferred land could be used within the meaning of section 106(1)(c).

Transfers of land and unilateral obligations

Certain problems with attempts to provide for the transfer of land in a unilateral planning obligation were identified in *Wimpey Homes Holdings Ltd v Secretary of State for the Environment and Winchester City Council* [1993] JPL 919. In that case developers offered a unilateral undertaking to transfer land to the local planning authority with the intention that it should be used as public open space. They contemplated that the council would enter into covenants restricting the use of the land. The court held that this was not a valid planning obligation. The transfer of title pursuant to the undertaking did not itself impose a restriction on the development or use of the land. It was simply a first step towards the later imposition of a restriction by means of a covenant. In addition, the obligation to transfer was incomplete since the transfer depended on the council entering into covenants, and they had not done so. The judge expressed the view that a unilateral undertaking could not be used to force another party to accept title to land.

Having said this, a unilateral undertaking could validly contain a *Grampian*-style restriction preventing the landowner from carrying out any development on one site until another site had been transferred to the local planning authority.

5. Local authority obligations

Where a planning obligation is created unilaterally it can only impose obligations on the landowner making it. Where planning obligations are created by agreement it is possible for the local planning authority itself to undertake to perform certain obligations—*e.g.* to carry out the infrastructure works being paid for by the developer. Any local authority obligation will be enforceable by the landowner and his successor in title.

A local planning authority can enter into a planning obligation in respect of land owned by another public authority—for example with the county council as education authority.

In entering into such obligations a local planning authority cannot fetter the future exercise of its statutory powers. Thus it cannot restrict its freedom to approve or reject future proposals for development[4] or to designate an area as a conservation area[5].

6. Examples of inappropriate planning obligations

In an appeal decision noted at [1994] JPL 493 the Secretary of State gave guidance on matters that were not appropriate for inclusion in a planning obligation accompanying a planning permission for mineral extraction. He held that provisions of the following kinds should not be included in a planning obligation:

- provision covering the setting up of a site liaison committee;
- provision establishing an approved route for HGVs using the site;
- undertaking by developer not to claim compensation in the event that an existing planning permission was revoked;
- undertaking by developer not to undertake development permitted by an existing permission; and
- undertaking by developer not to submit an application for a brickmaking factory.

[4] *Stringer* v *Ministry of Housing and Local Government* [1970] 1 WLR 1281.
[5] *Windsor and Maidenhead Royal BC* v *Brandrose Investments Ltd* [1983] 1 WLR 509.

Benefits Offered in Planning Obligations

CHAPTER 12

Benefits Offered in Planning Obligations

Introduction

In recent years there has been an increasing tendency for local planning authorities to seek, and for developers to offer, by way of planning obligations, substantial public benefits in return for grants of planning permission. Often the benefits have included offers to meet the cost of infrastructure works that would otherwise have been met from the public purse. In three celebrated recent cases the higher courts have had to consider what kind of benefits local planning authorities can legitimately seek to extract before granting planning permission, and the kinds of benefits offered that can properly be taken into account in deciding whether to grant planning permission.

The law in this area is by no means straightforward. The situation is impinged on by a number of discrete considerations, namely:

- The rules of validity of planning obligations
  A planning obligation that complies with these rules (see Chap 11) is legally valid, and creates a legally enforceable obligation binding on the landowner and his successors in title. However, because of constraints on how planning authorities can exercise their statutory powers, some valid planning obligations may have to be ignored when decisions on the granting of planning permissions are made.

- Government policy on planning obligations
  This is set out in Circular 16/91. Crucially this says that local planning authorities can only seek benefits from developers by means of planning obligations where such benefits are necessitated by the proposed development, and are proportionate to the development. This guidance has nothing to do with the legal validity of planning obligations and covers quite different matters from those discussed in Chapter 11.

- The validity of planning permissions granted on the strength of the offer of benefits in a planning obligation
  This involves investigation of the considerations ("material considerations") that planning authorities can properly take into

account when deciding whether to grant planning permission for a particular development. A planning obligation which is legally valid will not necessarily be a material consideration.

Conversely, while local planning authorities must always have regard to Government policy, the courts have held that local planning authorities are entitled to treat as material considerations offers of benefits that do not comply with the guidance in Circular 16/91.

● Approach taken by local planning authorities
Development control policies may provide that planning permission for certain types of development will be refused unless certain kinds of benefit are offered by developers by means of planning obligation.

The tests of legal validity of planning obligations are set out in Chapter 11. This chapter considers the remaining three considerations, and the recent case law relevant to them.

Requirements of Circular 16/91

Government policy on the use of planning obligations is contained in Circular 16/91 (set out in full in Appendix 2). The Circular is concerned with the kinds of benefits that it is legitimate for local planning authorities to seek before granting planning permission.

1. General approach

The Circular sets out the circumstances "in which certain types of benefit can reasonably be sought in connection with a grant of planning permission". These circumstances will be taken into account by the Secretary of State and inspectors in determining appeals (para B5). Local authorities are told to ensure that "the presence or absence of *extraneous* inducements or benefits does not influence their decision on the planning application" (para B5, emphasis added).

The guidance applies with equal force to planning obligations made by agreement and to those made unilaterally (para B12).

The Circular recognises that local planning authorities can legitimately seek to "secure modification or improvements" to submitted proposals by planning obligations, but prohibits "attempts to extract from developers payments in cash or in kind for purposes that are not directly related to the development proposed but are sought as 'the price of planning permission'". It also prohibits "offers from developers to a local authority that are not related to their development proposal" (para B3).

2. Particular requirements

Preference for conditions
In circumstances where it is reasonable to impose a condition or to require the developer to enter into a planning obligation "the imposition of a condition is preferable because it enables a developer to appeal to the Secretary of State". Also the terms of a condition should not be repeated in a planning obligation because this "would entail nugatory duplication and frustrate a developer's right of appeal" (para B6). (This guidance is repeated in para 12 of the Annex to Circular 11/95.)

Benefits offered must be relevant to planning and to the development

> "As with conditions ... planning obligations should only be sought where they are necessary to the granting of permission, relevant to planning and relevant to the development to be permitted. Unacceptable development should never be permitted because of unrelated benefits offered by the applicant, nor should an acceptable development be refused permission simply because the applicant is unable or unwilling to offer such unrelated benefits." (para B7)

The benefits offered can relate to land other than that covered by the permission, but there must be a direct relationship between the two, and the relationship must not be "too remote to be considered reasonable" (para B8).

Necessary to the granting of permission
The words "necessary to the granting of permission" are only used in paragraph B7. However, paragraph B8, which purports to explain "the test of the reasonableness of seeking a planning obligation", in fact further explains a test of necessity, stating that it will be reasonable to seek a planning obligation if the planning obligation:

> "(1) is *needed to enable the development to go ahead*, for example the provision of adequate access or car parking; or
>
> (2) in the case of financial payment, will contribute to meeting the cost of *providing such facilities* in the near future; or
>
> (3) is otherwise so directly related to the proposed development and to the use of the land after its completion, that *the development ought not to be permitted without it*, e.g. the provision ... of reasonable amounts of open space related to the development, or of social, educational, recreational, sporting or other community provision the need for which arises from the development; or

(4) is designed in the case of mixed development to secure an acceptable balance of uses; or to secure the implementation of local plan policies for a particular area or type of development ...; or

(5) is intended to offset the loss of or impact on any amenity or resource present on the site prior to development ..." (Emphasis added.)

Benefits offered must fairly and reasonably relate in scale and kind to the proposed development (proportionality)
Benefits in a planning obligation must be "fairly and reasonably related in scale and kind to the proposed development". Payments for infrastructure that would not have been necessary but for the development "should be directly related in scale to the benefit which the proposed development will derive from the facilities to be provided" (para B9).

Future maintenance costs
Planning obligations should not normally impose the cost of future maintenance of off-site facilities on developers. Exceptions may be made in the case of new highways or open space or landscaping principally of benefit to the development itself (para 10).

3. Application of the policy
The application of an earlier version of this policy (Circular 22/83), and in particular the test of necessity, was considered by the Court of Appeal in *Safeway* v *Secretary of State for the Environment and Greenwich LBC* [1991] JPL 966. In that case it was held that an Inspector had wrongly failed to take into account an offer of a contribution to traffic management measures. In the course of his judgment Parker LJ stated that the local planning authority, in applying the policy,

"had first to consider whether an application as it stood should be refused. If it so concluded it should then consider ... the acceptance of an offer that would negate the ground upon which it would, without the obligation, refuse permission ..." (p 968).

There is no doubt that this reasoning reflects the logic of Circular 16/91 also. The Circular does not provide useful guidance on what a local planning authority should do when offered a benefit that does not meet the test of necessity. This is part of the reason why the courts have had such difficulty with the test of necessity. As will be seen below, the position is that it would not be lawful for a local planning authority to close its mind to an offer of a benefit just because it did not meet the test of necessity. Moreover, it is not unlawful for a local planning authority to take an approach that is at variance with this policy.

For an example of a case where an inspector's decision to refuse planning permission because the developer had not offered a planning obligation that would have been justified by the terms of Circular 16/91 was upheld, see *Pickavance* v *Secretary of State for the Environment* [1994] JPL 459.

Recent case-law

As has been pointed out above, the legal limits on the validity of a planning obligation (discussed in Chap 11) have nothing to do with the terms of the Circular. This means that a local planning authority may be faced with an application for planning permission accompanied by a unilateral planning obligation which does not comply with the guidance in the Circular, but which is nevertheless legally valid.

In recent years this problem has arisen most acutely with regard to planning obligations offered by rival developers that do not meet the tests of necessity and proportionality in the Circular. Three recent cases have considered what local planning authorities may do when faced with such offers, and the extent to which local planning authorities can themselves seek benefits by means of planning obligations in their development control policies.

It is convenient to set out a brief summary of each case before considering the implications of the decisions.

- *R* v *Plymouth City Council ex p Plymouth and South Devon Co–Operative Society Ltd* (1993) 67 P&CR 78: A local planning authority was faced with three applications for supermarket development. Two of the proposals offered, by way of planning obligations, benefits that were not necessitated by the development proposed. The local planning authority gave permission for these two schemes and for a reduced version of the third scheme. The developer of the third scheme challenged the two other grants of planning permission on the basis that they had been made as a result of taking into account the offers of benefit, which should not have been regarded as material considerations.

  The Court of Appeal rejected the challenges, holding that the only tests for whether an offer of benefit was a material consideration were those set out in *Newbury DC* v *Secretary of State for the Environment* [1981] AC 578, namely that the benefit was relevant to planning, related to the development and was reasonable. There was no additional test of necessity or proportionality. The offers in this case met the tests of materiality.

The House of Lords in *Tesco* (see below) had difficulties with the application of the *Newbury* tests to planning obligations.

- *R v South Northamptonshire DC ex p Crest Homes plc* [1995] JPL 200: Structure plan policy made it clear that considerable extra development would have to take place at Towcester. The local planning authority took the view that considerable extra infrastructure would need to be provided to accommodate this development, and sought to secure contributions to the costs of such infrastructure from those likely to be involved in major developments. Consultation with such developers took place. In the course of this the local planning authority identified the infrastructure required and its total cost, and sought ways to relate the cost of providing this to individual proposals for development. It eventually settled on an approach which required developers to contribute a percentage of the additional land value arising by reason of the grant of planning permission to the costs of this infrastructure (20% in the case of residential development, and 17.5% in the case of commercial development). This approach was reflected in the local plan, the relevant policy in which stated that proposals for major development would be expected to make provision for related infrastructure and community facilities by means of planning obligations, and that such provision would normally take the form of financial contributions to on-site or off-site facilities.

  A developer (who had been involved in the consultations) challenged the policy and also certain planning permissions granted on the strength of planning obligations that made the appropriate financial contributions.

  The Court of Appeal rejected the challenges. It held that the policy was based on a genuine identification of the infrastructure requirements of Towcester as a whole, and on a genuine attempt to distribute the costs of this among the various developers, and was legitimate. Given the magnitude of the development catered for, the council was entitled to conclude that the formula produced a contribution from each development that fairly and reasonably related to the development and was not disproportionate.

- *Tesco Stores Ltd v Secretary of State for the Environment* [1995] JPL 581: This case concerned rival superstore proposals in Witney. A proposal made by Tesco was accompanied by an undertaking to fund a road link so as to relieve congestion in the town centre. This congestion would only have been worsened marginally by a new superstore. A rival proposal for a superstore did not include any offer of such funding. The Secretary of State refused planning permission for the Tesco proposal and gave permission to the rival. The Secretary of State concluded that Tesco's undertaking did not satisfy the tests of necessity and proportionality. Nevertheless (according to the House of Lords) he still regarded it as a material consideration, although giving it very little weight in his decision. Tesco challenged the refusal of planning permission.

The House of Lords dismissed the challenge. It held that a planning obligation which related to the relevant development was a "material consideration" which has to be taken into account by the decision–maker in deciding whether to grant planning permission, and that there was no legal requirement that planning obligations should satisfy tests of necessity or proportionality. The planning obligation offered by Tesco was accordingly a material consideration which the Secretary of State had rightly taken into account. However, the weight to be attached to any material consideration was entirely a matter for the decision-maker, and the Secretary of State was therefore entitled to give the planning obligation offered by Tesco little weight. The Secretary of State was entitled to adopt a policy (expressed in Circular 16/91) that planning obligations should only be considered to the extent that they offered benefits that were necessitated by and proportionate to the development concerned.

The main judgment was given by Lord Keith of Kinkel, with whom all the other Lords agreed. Lord Hoffman added some interesting observations of his own (see pages 122–123 below).

Validity of planning permission granted on strength of offer of benefit in planning obligation

1. Planning obligation as material consideration

In deciding whether to grant or refuse planning permission, a planning authority has to have regard to all "material considerations". This requirement is specifically set out in section 70(2) of the 1990 Act. In addition, it is a general principle of public law that decision-makers must not ignore material (*i.e.* relevant) considerations in reaching their decisions. Conversely, decision-makers must pay no regard to irrelevant considerations. The weight that the decision-maker attaches to any particular material consideration is not a matter that the courts will investigate.

If the offer of benefits in a planning obligation is properly to be regarded as a "material consideration" it must be considered by the local planning authority. The mere fact that a planning obligation is legally valid (see Chap 11) does not make it a material consideration. A local planning authority may therefore be faced with a legally valid planning obligation which it has to ignore in reaching its decision on whether to grant planning permission.

Tesco decides that, provided that there is a connection between the planning obligation and the development that is not *de minimis*, the obligation is a material consideration in the decision whether to grant permission (see [1995] JPL at p 589 per Lord Keith). The *Newbury* tests were said not to be particularly helpful for the purposes of assessing whether a planning obligation could properly be regarded as a material consideration. Lord Keith observed that a planning obligation that had nothing to do with proposed development or which failed to overcome valid planning objections to a proposal would not be a material consideration.

In *Tesco* itself, there was a tenuous relationship between the obligation and the development. As a result, the House of Lords held that the obligation was a material consideration, and therefore had to be taken into account by the Secretary of State. The House of Lords stressed that the weight to be attached to the consideration was entirely a matter for the decision-maker.

Plymouth provides useful guidance on the circumstances in which benefits will be regarded as related to the development. In that case the following offers were said to relate to the development:

1. *£0.8 million towards providing park and ride facilities elsewhere in Plymouth.* This was said to relate to the development because these facilities, by reducing vehicular traffic, would counter the traffic generated by the superstore (Russell LJ at 67 P&CR, pp 82–3) and would reduce traffic that might otherwise conflict with traffic using the superstore (Hoffman LJ at pp 90–91).
2. *Offer of £1 million towards providing infrastructure for a new industrial site.* This was said to relate to the development because the relevant superstore was built on land allocated for industrial purposes. The bringing forward of other industrial land could be regarded as compensation for this loss.
3. *Offer of facilities on or adjacent to superstore sites (including a tourist centre and a bird watching hide).* These were said to relate to the development because they were provided on site and made the development more attractive (Russell LJ at p 82) and benefited the developer as well as the local community (Hoffman LJ at p 90).

The fact that a benefit is included in the application will not of itself mean that sufficient connection with the development is necessarily established (*Barber* v *Secretary of State for the Environment* [1991] JPL 559).

2. No tests of necessity and proportionality

Tesco, following *Plymouth*, holds that there is no legal requirement for the validity or materiality of a planning obligation that the obligation should satisfy a test of necessity or proportionality. These tests do not derive from the Act ([1995] JPL at p 595 per Lord Hoffman) but are entirely a matter of the Secretary of State's policy. Whether a benefit offered is necessary and proportionate merely goes to the weight to be attached to the planning obligation as a material consideration. Were the courts to impose a legal test of necessity they would have to investigate the planning merits of a scheme (to ascertain what objections any planning obligation would have to overcome), something they are quite unwilling to do. Lord Keith observed that the test of necessity was merely an indication of when weight should be attached to an obligation ([1995] JPL at p 589).

As Lord Hoffman pointed out, tests of necessity and proportionality derive from the general policy of a presumption in favour of granting planning permission. This general policy plainly makes it inappropriate to require a planning obligation to be given unless that obligation is needed to overcome what would otherwise be a reason for refusing permission. While this general policy is plainly within the scope of the discretion conferred on the Secretary of State by the 1990 Act, there is no requirement to have such a policy. It would be perfectly open, he said, to the Secretary of State to adopt a policy that planning permission should only be granted where good reason could be shown, which might include "the willingness of the developer to provide related external benefits" ([1995] JPL at pp 595–6). Having said this, Lord Hoffman made it clear that, if a planning authority found a development to be acceptable on its merits, a decision that a planning obligation should nevertheless be required to achieve public benefits would probably be unreasonable in a *Wednesbury* sense ([1995] JPL at p 599). (See page 105 above.)

Approaches taken by local planning authorities

I. Competitions

It is important to appreciate the context in which recent problems concerning planning obligations have arisen. Both *Tesco* and *Plymouth* concerned "competitions" for planning permission, where one or more rivals for planning permission for development offer additional benefits by means of planning obligation. As Lord Hoffman pointed out, when faced with making a choice between rival proposals, it would certainly be appropriate for a planning authority to take into account differences in benefits provided on-site, and it would be difficult to take a different approach to benefits provided off-site. An approach based on the presumption in favour of granting planning permission "does not yield an easy answer" ([1995] JPL at p 596). In such a case "it may be perfectly rational to choose the proposal which offers the greatest public benefit in terms of both the development itself and related external benefits" even if these benefits were not necessitated by the development and were not proportionate to its impact. The decisions of the local planning authority in that case were taken in pursuance of "a policy of attempting to obtain the maximum public benefit", not the policy to be found in Circular 16/91, but nevertheless an approach the local planning authority was entitled to take. Similarly, it would have been open to the Secretary of State in *Tesco* to adopt such an approach, and to have "given the planning permission to Tesco on the grounds that its proposal offered the greater public benefit" ([1995] JPL at pp 600–601). Lord Keith also made it clear that the local planning authority was not legally bound to follow the Secretary of State's policy.

2. Role of Circular 16/91
It must be pointed out that the policy in Circular 16/91 is itself a material consideration in any decision which concerns planning obligations. Thus, while planning authorities are entitled to take a different approach, they cannot simply ignore the Circular. To do so would be to ignore a material consideration.

3. *Crest Homes*
The challenges in *Crest Homes* included a challenge to the policy that required those proposing to carry out any major development to make a contribution to the relevant infrastructure costs. In addition, although the local plan policy itself did not mention specific percentages of enhanced land values, the court also considered this aspect of the approach. The situation in *Crest Homes* was not one of a competition.

The court held that it was legitimate to have an approach of this kind provided that it only sought benefits which fairly and reasonably related to the proposed development, and that the benefits that were sought were proportionate. These tests were based on the tests for the materiality of planning obligations (the question considered in *Tesco*). It was said that proportionality might be a "subhead" of the second *Newbury* test. This approach is not wholly consistent with *Tesco* which eschews both *Newbury* and a test of proportionality.

The true significance of the decision in *Crest Homes* is not the legal principle but its application to the policy in question. The upshot of the policy was that planning permission for major developments would not be granted unless the developers paid a proportion of the enhanced land value to the local planning authority. Henry LJ made the point that in other factual contexts the formula would constitute an unlawful development land tax ([1995] JPL at p 209). In the circumstances of the case it was lawful because it represented a bona fide and genuine attempt to secure from developers monies that would be spent on providing infrastructure made necessary by the various developments. Henry LJ accepted that it was legitimate for the council to consider the infrastructure requirements of Towcester as a whole, and to attempt to spread the cost of this over all the major developments contemplated. The percentage approach had been found to be the only practicable way to fix the contribution of individual developers. For this reason it was possible to say that the benefits that would be derived from the payment of the contributions fairly and reasonably related to the developments permitted, and that the amount of the contribution could not be regarded as excessive.

Henry LJ made two other points of importance.

First, "with some diffidence" he rejected the contention that, at the time of the challenge, it had to be certain that the monies payable under such a planning obligation would be applied to pay for the relevant infrastructure. He said that it would be sufficient if the contribution was one which the local planning authority could regard as a genuine pre–estimate of the developer's proper contribution to the related infrastructure. If, later, it transpired that the money had not been so applied the developer might have "other remedies" ([1995] JPL at pp 208–9).

Secondly, Henry LJ accepted that the council's policy had proper regard to Circular 16/91 ([1995] JPL at pp 209–10). In particular the policy "easily satisfied" the test of reasonableness in paragraph B8 (which effectively sets out the test of necessity) and the test of proportionality in paragraph B9. "On the vexed question of necessity, [the local planning authority was] quite entitled to take the unified view that the expansion of Towcester, even if inevitable, should not take place unless the major developers contributed to the costs of the infrastructure related to the expansion and to the individual major developments comprising it."

Enforcement of Planning Obligations

CHAPTER 13

Enforcement of Planning Obligations

Persons bound by planning obligations

By section 106(3):

> a planning obligation is enforceable by the authority ...
>
> (a) against the person entering into the obligation; and
> (b) against any person deriving title from that person.

This means that anyone who buys or otherwise acquires the original party's interest will be bound by the obligation. It also means that anyone who has an interest derived from the original party's interest is bound. Thus, if the original party is the freeholder, any third party rights (for example tenancies or easements) that he thereafter creates will be bound, provided that the obligation is registered as a Local Land Charge— see Chapter 11, page 109. Where a landowner has created a third party right before entering into the planning obligation the third party is not bound unless he himself enters into the planning obligation.

A landowner creating a planning obligation cannot bind an interest that does not derive from his title. Thus, for example, a planning obligation entered into by a tenant will not bind the freeholder.

It follows that a planning obligation will offer no satisfactory safeguard over the future use of land unless the original covenantee has sufficient title in the land. Paragraph B12 of Circular 16/91 provides that, at an appeal, if the developer's title has not been demonstrated, the inspector may seek evidence of that title.

Unless express provision is made to the contrary, the original landowner will remain liable for breaches of the planning obligation even after he has sold his interest. However, section 106(4) provides that:

> the instrument by which a planning obligation is entered into may provide that a person shall not be bound by the obligation in respect of any period during which he no longer has an interest in the land.

Enforcement

A planning obligation is enforceable by the local planning authority identified in it. In non–metropolitan areas both district and county councils have planning functions. Both can therefore be identified in planning obligations as authorities able to enforce the obligations.

1. Enforcement by injunction

Planning obligations are enforceable by injunction (s 106(5)). Occasions may arise when the requirements of a planning obligation mirror the ordinary requirements of planning control. The mere fact that a breach of planning control is the subject of an appeal will not prevent an interlocutory injunction from being granted to restrain breach of a planning obligation. Thus, in *Avon CC* v *Millard* [1986] JPL 211 (a case concerning an old section 52 agreement) it was held that an injunction would be the normal remedy for a local planning authority faced with breach of such an agreement (because damages would be an inadequate remedy) and that there was no requirement that ordinary enforcement measures should first be exhausted[1].

2. Direct action

In addition, where the planning obligation creates a positive obligation to carry out operations, the local planning authority can take direct action against the land affected. Section 106(6)–(7) provides:

> (6) **Without prejudice to subsection (5)** [dealing with injunctions], **if there is a breach of a requirement in a planning obligation to carry out any operations in, on, under or over the land to which the obligation relates, the authority by whom the obligation is enforceable may—**
>
> > (a) **enter the land and carry out the operations; and**
> > (b) **recover from the person or persons against whom the obligation is enforceable any expenses reasonably incurred by them in doing so.**
>
> (7) **Before an authority exercise their power under subsection (6)(a) they shall give not less than 21 days' notice of their intention to do so to any person against whom the planning obligation is enforceable.**

Notice of intention to enter the land has to be served on "any person against whom the planning obligation is enforceable". Where the original

---

[1] See also *Tower Hamlets LBC* v *Stanton Rubber and Plastics Ltd* [1990] JPL 512, a case where an interlocutory injunction was granted even though an appeal to the Secretary of State against the equivalent condition was pending.

landowner has sold or burdened his interest, there may be several people in this position, as explained above. The costs incurred by the local planning authority in carrying out the operations will be recoverable against any of these persons under subsection (6)(b).

Section 106(12) makes provision for regulations to be made to provide for the charging of the costs of carrying out such works against the land itself. To date no such regulations have been made.

By section106(8) **any person who wilfully obstructs a person acting in the exercise of a power under subsection (6)(a) shall be guilty of an offence and liable on summary conviction to a fine not exceeding level 3 on the standard scale**. The current level 3 fine is £1,000.

Modification and Discharge of Planning Obligations

CHAPTER 14

Modification and Discharge of Planning Obligations

Introduction

Under the normal law of real property, covenants binding on land can be modified or discharged only by the agreement of the parties involved or by order of the Lands Tribunal on an application made under section 84 of the Law of Property Act 1925. Orders under section 84 can only be made on certain specified grounds, and may involve the payment of compensation. Until the changes brought about by the Planning and Compensation Act 1991 this regime also applied to planning agreements under the original section 106 and its predecessor, section 52 of the Town and Country Planning Act 1971.

The Planning and Compensation Act 1991 introduced a new section 106, and with it the concept of the planning obligation. It also introduced a special method for securing the modification or discharge of such obligations, set out in sections 106A and 106B, and provided that section 84 of the Law of Property Act should have no application to planning obligations (s 106A(10)).

In addition planning obligations can be modified and discharged by agreement.

Modification and discharge by agreement

A planning obligation can be modified or discharged by agreement between the relevant local planning authority and the person or persons against whom the obligation is enforceable (s 106A(1)). Such agreement has to be by deed (s 106A(2)). The persons against whom a planning obligation may be enforceable are discussed in Chapter 13. Planning obligations bind the land of the person creating the obligation, and can make provision for the landowner's liability to cease when his interest in the land ceases. It follows that the parties to an agreement to modify or discharge a planning obligation may be different from the parties who originally executed the deed.

Section 106A(1) applies to planning obligations created both unilaterally and by agreement.

Modification or discharge by application to local planning authority

The new procedure can only be used after five years have elapsed from the making of the planning obligation, and involves applying to the local planning authority for the modification or discharge sought. There exists a right of appeal to the Secretary of State against the local planning authority's decision.

1. Application to local planning authority
Section 106A(3) provides that:

> A person against whom a planning obligation is enforceable may, at any time after the expiry of the relevant period, apply to the local planning authority by whom the obligation is enforceable for the obligation
>
> (a) to have effect subject to such modification as may be specified in the application; or
> (b) to be discharged.

The **relevant period** is five years from the date the planning obligation was made, or such other period as may be prescribed.

On such an application the local planning authority may determine, under section 106A(6):

> (a) that the planning obligation shall continue to have effect without modification;
> (b) if the obligation no longer serves a useful purpose, that it should be discharged; or
> (c) if the obligation continues to serve a useful purpose, but would serve that purpose equally as well if it had effect subject to the modifications specified in the application, that it shall have effect subject to those modifications.

2. The applicant
Any of the persons against whom the planning obligation is enforceable can make such an application. The suggested modification can involve changes that make the planning obligation more onerous. However, section 106A(5) provides that **an application under subsection (3) for the modification of a planning obligation may not specify a**

modification imposing an obligation on any other person against whom the obligation is enforceable. Thus an applicant cannot, by seeking a modification, impose new or more onerous obligations on a third party also bound by the planning obligation. For such a third party to be bound, he must be joined as an applicant for the modification.

3. Procedure

The procedure for applying for a modification or discharge of a planning obligation is laid down in the Town and Country Planning (Modification and Discharge of Planning Obligations) Regulations 1992. The application must be made on a form provided by the local planning authority (reg 3). The applicant must notify any other person against whom the planning obligation is enforceable (reg 4). The local planning authority must publicise the application and invite representations. These publicity requirements are greater than those which apply on the initial creation of the planning obligation.

The local planning authority must give notice of its decision within eight weeks, or such longer period as may be agreed with the applicant (s 106A(7); reg 6(2)).

4. The decision of the local planning authority

In considering the application the local planning authority must decide whether the planning obligation continues to "serve a useful purpose". If it does not, the authority must discharge the obligation. If it does, the authority must consider whether that purpose would be served equally well by any suggested modification. If a suggested modification would serve this purpose, the local planning authority should modify the planning obligation accordingly. If it would not, the local planning authority should decline to modify the planning obligation. The local planning authority must confine its attention to such modifications as are sought in the application. It cannot impose a modification of its own devising.

Where the local planning authority determines that the planning obligation should not be modified, it must state the reasons for its decision (reg 6(3)).

Where the local planning authority decides to modify the planning obligation, the modified planning obligation is enforceable as of the date of the authority's decision (s 106A(8)).

5. Appeal to the Secretary of State

A right of appeal to the Secretary of State exists if the local planning authority either fails to determine the application within the eight-week period (or such extended period as the parties agree) or determines that the planning obligation should continue to have effect without modification (s 106B(1)). Where an appeal is made because the local planning authority has failed to make a decision within the requisite time, the local authority is treated as if it had determined that the planning obligation should continue to have effect unmodified (s 106B(2)).

The appeal must be made within six months of the decision of the local planning authority, or of the expiry of the eight-week period (or such longer period as is agreed). The Secretary of State has a discretion to extend the six-month period for appealing (reg 7(1)).

The appeal is made using a prescribed form, and must be accompanied by copies of the application to the local planning authority, the certificate that accompanied the application, the deed creating the planning obligation, any correspondence with the local planning authority, and notice of any decision of the local planning authority (reg 7(1) and (2)).

Section 106B(5) provides that:

> before determining the appeal the Secretary of State shall, if either the applicant or the authority so wish, give each of them an opportunity of appearing before and being heard by a person appointed by the Secretary of State for the purpose.

The Secretary of State's powers on an appeal are the same as the local planning authority's powers when considering an application (see page 132 above). Thus he must consider whether the planning obligation continues to serve a useful purpose, and if not, must discharge it. If he decides that it does continue to serve a useful purpose he must consider whether any modifications suggested in the original application would serve that purpose equally well. If he so decides he must modify the planning obligation accordingly.

Appeals to the Secretary of State will be determined by an inspector (see reg 8 and Sched 6 to the 1990 Act) unless the Secretary of State recovers jurisdiction to himself (see Sched 6, para 3).

APPENDICES

APPENDIX 1

Circular 11/95 – The Use of Conditions in Planning Permissions[1]

1.   DOE Circular 1/85 (WO 1/85) gave advice about the use of planning conditions. Much of that advice remains relevant, but it contains a number of references to legislation which has been replaced or amended since the Circular was published. This Circular brings these references up to date and incorporates additional policy guidance issued since 1985, for example, in Planning Policy Guidance Notes: in particular, it reflects guidance on the use of conditions in respect of transport, retail development, contaminated land, noise and affordable housing. Additional advice has been included in respect of design and landscape, lorry routeing, "granny" annexes, staff accommodation, access for disabled people, holiday occupancy, and nature conservation/endangered species (see Index for details). The Circular also takes account of court decisions and includes an expanded Appendix containing "model" conditions.

2.   The power to impose conditions when granting planning permission is very wide. If used properly, conditions can enhance the quality of development and enable many development proposals to proceed where it would otherwise have been necessary to refuse planning permission. The objectives of planning, however, are best served when that power is exercised in such a way that conditions are clearly seen to be fair, reasonable and practicable. This Circular, with its Annex, sets out guidance on how this can be achieved.

3.   Paragraphs 14-42 of the Annex, stress that conditions should only be imposed where they are both necessary and reasonable, as well as enforceable, precise and relevant both to planning and to the development to be permitted. Attention is particularly drawn to paragraphs 15-17 which advise that in considering whether a condition is necessary authorities should ask themselves whether planning permission would have to be refused if the requirements of that condition were not imposed. If it would not, then the condition needs special and precise justification. Attention is also drawn to paragraph 29 of the Annex, alerting authorities to a judgment with important implications for enforcing planning conditions.

4.   It is essential that the operation of the planning system should command public confidence. The sensitive use of conditions can improve development

[1]Issued 20 July 1995 by the Department of the Environment and the Welsh Office (Circular 35/95).

control and enhance that confidence. The use of conditions in an unreasonable way, however, so that it proves impracticable or inexpedient to enforce them, will damage such confidence and should be avoided.

5.   When applications come to appeal, the Secretaries of State or Planning Inspectors welcome reasoned suggestions from the parties as to conditions which they would find acceptable if permission were granted. Such suggestions will be fully examined and may or may not be adopted, but conditions will not be imposed if they are considered to be invalid or if they are unacceptable on policy grounds.

6.   Since July 1992, local planning authorities have been able to ensure compliance with many planning conditions by serving a breach of condition notice. Guidance about this type of notice is given in Annex 2 to DOE Circular 17/92 (WO 38/92). If a valid breach of condition notice is contravened, the resulting offence is open to summary prosecution. But the prosecution's case must always be proved on the criminal standard of proof ("beyond reasonable doubt"). Consequently, if the breach of condition notice procedure is to operate effectively, planning conditions must be formulated precisely. In the event of prosecution, the Magistrates' Court will then have no doubt about exactly what is required in order to comply with the terms of a planning condition.

7.   This Circular does not include specific advice on policy on the use of planning conditions for the specialist subject of minerals workings or for most developments relating to waste management. Advice on conditions applicable to mineral developments is contained in the series of Minerals Planning Guidance Notes (MPGs) and on waste management development control in PPG 23: Planning and Pollution Control (England only).

8.   This Circular repeats and brings up to date existing advice, and should therefore have no effect on local government manpower or expenditure.

9.   Department of the Environment Circular 1/85 (WO 1/85) is now cancelled.

RICHARD JONES, *Assistant Secretary*
W P RODERICK, *Assistant Secretary*

Index to Annex [references are to paragraph numbers]

Annex

References below to "model" are to the model conditions shown in Appendix A.

Powers

Summary of powers
1.   Conditions may only be imposed within the powers available. Advice on these powers is given below. This advice is intended to be a guide, and it must be stressed that it is not definitive. An authoritative statement of the law can only be made by the courts. The principal powers are in Sections 70, 72, 73, 73A, and Schedule 5 to the Town and Country Planning Act 1990 (referred to below as "the Act"). Sections 91 and 92 of the Act require the imposition of time-limiting conditions on grants of planning permission (see paragraphs 53-56 below). Powers to impose conditions are also conferred on the Secretaries of State or their Inspectors by sections 77, 79 and 177 of, and Schedule 6 to, the Act. Unless the permission otherwise provides, planning permission runs with the land and any conditions imposed on the permission will bind successors in title. In some areas there may also be powers under local Acts which complement or vary the powers in the 1990 Act.

2.   Section 70(1)(a) of the Act enables the local planning authority in granting planning permission to impose "such conditions as they think fit". This power is not, however, as wide as it appears, and has to be interpreted in the light of court decisions.

Powers for conditions on land outside application site and temporary permissions
3.   Section 72(1)(a)amplifies the general power in section 70(1)(a) in two ways. It makes clear that the local planning authority may impose conditions regulating the development or use of land under the control of the applicant even if it is outside the site which is the subject of the application. (The courts have held that the question whether land is under control of an applicant is a matter to be determined according to the facts of the particular case, and is not dependent on the existence of a freehold or leasehold interest: only such control over the land is needed as is required to enable the developer to comply with the condition). The section also makes clear that the local planning authority may grant planning permission for a specified period only.

Power to vary or remove the effect of conditions
4.   Section 73 of the Act provides for applications for planning permission to develop land without complying with conditions previously imposed on a

planning permission. The local planning authority can grant such permission unconditionally or subject to different conditions, or they can refuse the application if they decide the original condition(s) should continue. The original planning permission will continue to subsist whatever the outcome of the application under section 73. Section 73 will not apply if the period in the previous condition limiting the duration within which the development could begin has now expired without the development having begun.[2]

5.   Section 73A of the Act provides, among other things, for retrospective planning applications to be made in respect of development which has been carried out without permission, and for applications for planning permission to authorise development which has been carried out without complying with some planning condition to which it was subject. Special consideration may need to be given to conditions imposed on planning permissions granted under section 73A. For example, the standard time-limiting condition will not be appropriate where development has begun before planning permission has been granted.

Other constraints

Policy and other constraints
6.   The limits of the enabling powers are not the only constraints on the use of conditions. Conditions should normally be consistent with national planning policies as expressed in Government Circulars, Planning Policy Guidance notes, Minerals Policy Guidance Notes and other published material. They should also normally accord with the provisions of development plans and other policies of local planning authorities. Where a certain kind of condition is specifically endorsed by a development plan policy, however, it is still necessary to consider whether it is justified in the particular circumstances of the proposed development. In general, conditions which duplicate the effect of other legislation should not be imposed (see paragraphs 21-23 below).

Practice

Role of informal discussions
7.   Even before an application is made, informal discussions between an applicant and the local planning authority are very helpful. They can allow the applicant to formulate the details of a project so as to take full account of the authority's requirements, and assist the authority in making sure that those requirements are reasonable in the light of the development proposed. They can

---

[2]However, it was held by Pill J in *R v Secretary of State for the Environment ex parte Corby BC* [1994] 1 PLR 38 that an application can be made under section 73 after the period for approval of reserved matters on an outline planning permission has expired but before the expiry of the period for commencement of development.

reduce the need for conditions, explore the possible terms of conditions which remain necessary, and ensure that these are tailored to the circumstances of the case.

"Standard conditions"

8.   The compilation by local planning authorities of lists of model conditions can be of great benefit. They can improve the consistency of decisions, the use of staff resources, and the speed with which planning applications are processed. They may also, however, encourage the use of conditions as a matter of routine, without the careful assessment of the need for each condition which every applicant should be entitled to expect. Model conditions therefore need to be treated with caution. Such lists can usefully be made available locally so that developers can take account of possible conditions at an early stage in drawing up their proposals, but should contain a warning that they are not comprehensive and that conditions will always be devised or adapted where appropriate to suit the particular circumstances of a case.

Policies about conditions in structure and local plans

9.   Where appropriate, development plans should specify the policies which the authority propose to implement regularly by means of planning conditions. (For further policy advice and guidance see paragraph 5.55 of PPG12: Development Plans and Regional Planning Guidance (Paragraph 5.54 of PPG12 (Wales)—Development Plans and Strategic Planning Guidance in Wales)).

Reasons

10.   It is for the local planning authority, in the first instance, to judge on the facts of the case, whether a particular development proposal should be approved subject to planning conditions. By virtue of the requirements in Article 22 of the Town and Country Planning (General Development Procedure) Order 1995, that an authority deciding to grant permission subject to conditions shall state the reasons for their decision, reasons must be given for the imposition of every condition. Reasons such as "to comply with the policies of the Council", "to secure the proper planning of the area" or "to maintain control over the development" are vague, and can suggest that the condition in question has no proper justification. The phrase "to protect amenity" can also be obscure, and will often need amplification. If the reasons for the imposition of conditions are clearly explained, developers will be better able to understand the need for them and to comply with them. The likelihood of proper and acceptable conditions being challenged on appeal, so that development proposals are held up, will also be diminished.

Notes of "informatives"

11.   Sometimes local planning authorities will wish to give guidance to an applicant for outline planning permission as to the kind of details of reserved

matters which they would find acceptable (see paragraphs 45 and 46 below). On occasions, a local planning authority may wish to draw the attention of an applicant to other statutory consents (e.g. listed building consent or a footpath diversion order) which must be obtained before development can commence. This should not be done by imposing a condition: instead a note may be appended to the planning permission. A note may also be desirable to draw the attention of the applicant to his or her right to make an application to vary or remove a condition under section 73 of the Act, or indeed for other purposes.

Planning obligations

12. It may be possible to overcome a planning objection to a development proposal equally well by imposing a condition on the planning permission or by entering into a planning obligation under section 106 of the Act. The Secretaries of State consider that in such cases the local planning authority should impose a condition rather than seek to deal with the matter by means of a planning obligation. This is because the imposition of restrictions by means of a planning obligation deprives the developer of the opportunity of seeking to have the restrictions varied or removed by an application or appeal under Part III of the Act if they are or become inappropriate or too onerous. It should be noted, however, that section 106A of the Act allows a developer to apply to the local planning authority to discharge or modify a planning obligation after the expiry of five years after the obligation is entered into—for further advice see DOE Circular 28/92 (WO 66/92).

13. Where conditions are imposed on a planning permission they should not be duplicated by a planning obligation. Permission cannot be granted subject to a condition that the applicant enters into a planning obligation under section 106 of the Act or an agreement under other powers.

Tests

Six tests for conditions

14. On a number of occasions the courts have laid down the general criteria for the validity of planning conditions. In addition to satisfying the court's criteria for validity, the Secretaries of State take the view that conditions should not be imposed unless they are both necessary and effective, and do not place unjustifiable burdens on applicants. As a matter of policy, conditions should only be imposed where they satisfy all of the tests described in paragraphs 14-42. In brief, these explain that conditions should be

    (i) necessary;
    (ii) relevant to planning;

(iii) relevant to the development to be permitted;

(iv) enforceable;

 (v) precise; and

(vi) reasonable in all other respects.

Need for a condition

15. In considering whether a particular condition is necessary, authorities should ask themselves whether planning permission would have to be refused if that condition were not to be imposed. If it would not, then the condition needs special and precise justification. The argument that a condition will do no harm is no justification for its imposition: as a matter of policy, a condition ought not to be imposed unless there is a definite need for it. The same principles, of course, must be applied in dealing with applications for the removal of a condition under section 73 or section 73A: a condition should not be retained unless there are sound and clear-cut reasons for doing so.

16. In some cases a condition is clearly unnecessary, such as where it would repeat provisions in another condition imposed on the same permission. In other cases the lack of need may be less obvious, and it may help to ask whether it would be considered expedient to enforce against a breach—if not, then the condition may well be unnecessary.

17. Conditions should be tailored to tackle specific problems, rather than impose unjustified controls. In so far as a condition is wider in its scope than is necessary to achieve the desired objective, it will fail the test of need. Where an extension to a dwellinghouse in a particular direction would be unacceptable, for example, a condition on the permission for its erection should specify that, and not simply remove all rights to extend the building. Permissions should not be overloaded with conditions, however: it might be appropriate for example, to impose on a permission in a conservation or other sensitive area a requirement that all external details and materials should be in complete accordance with the approved plans and specifications, rather than recite a long list of architectural details one by one.

Completion of development
18. Conditions requiring development to be carried out in its entirety, or in complete accordance with the approved plans, often fail the test of need by requiring more than is needed to deal with the problem they are designed to solve. If what is really wanted is simply to ensure that some particular feature or features of the development are actually provided or are finished in a certain way, specific conditions to this end (for example, model conditions 17 and 22) are far preferable to a general requirement.

19. The absence of a specific condition does not prevent enforcement action being taken against development which differs materially from the approved design. However, it may well be easier for local planning authorities to enforce compliance with a condition that has been breached, than to enforce on the basis of a material variation from the approved plans or description of development. Where an application includes information, for example on likely hours of working, which significantly influence the planning decision, it may therefore be appropriate to include a specific condition to ensure compliance with the restrictions.

Relevance to planning

20. A condition which has no relevance to planning is *ultra vires*. A condition that the first occupants of dwellings must be drawn from the local authority's housing waiting list, for example, would be improper because it was meant to meet the ends of the local authority as housing authority and was not imposed for planning reasons (but see paragraph 97 below). Although a condition can quite properly require the provision of open space to serve the permitted development (as part of a housing estate for example) it would be *ultra vires* if it required the open space to be dedicated to the public; other conditions affecting land ownership (requiring, for example, that the land shall not be disposed of except as a whole) would similarly be *ultra vires*.

Other planning controls
21. Some matters are the subject of specific control elsewhere in planning legislation, for example advertisement control, listed building consent or tree preservation. If these controls are relevant to the development the authority should normally rely on them, and not impose conditions on a grant of planning permission to achieve the purposes of a separate system of control (but on trees note paragraph 51 below).

Non-planning controls
22. Other matters are subject to control under separate legislation, yet also of concern to the planning system. A condition which duplicates the effect of other controls will normally be unnecessary, and one whose requirements conflict with those of other controls will be *ultra vires* because it is unreasonable. For example, a planning condition would not normally be appropriate to control the level of emissions from a proposed development where they are subject to pollution control, but may be needed to address the impact of the emissions to the extent that they might have land-use implications and are not controlled by the appropriate pollution control authority (for further advice on conditions and pollution see paragraphs 3.23-3,28 of PPG23: Planning and Pollution Control) (England only). A condition cannot be justified on the grounds that the local

planning authority is not the body responsible for exercising a concurrent control, and therefore cannot ensure that it will be exercised properly. Nor can a condition be justified on the grounds that a concurrent control is not permanent but is subject to expiry and renewal (as, for example, with certain licences). Nor, as a matter of policy, should conditions be imposed in order to avoid a liability to pay compensation under other legislation. Even where a condition does not actually duplicate or conflict with another control, differences in requirements can cause confusion, and it will be desirable as far as possible to avoid solving problems by the use of conditions instead of, or as well as, by another more specific control.

23. Where other controls are also available, a condition may, however, be needed when the considerations material to the exercise of the two systems of control are substantially different, since it might be unwise in these circumstances to rely on the alternative control being exercised in the manner or to the degree needed to secure planning objectives. Conditions may also be needed to deal with circumstances for which a concurrent control is unavailable. A further case where conditions may be justified will be where they can prevent development being carried out in a manner which would be likely to give rise to onerous requirements under other powers at a later stage (*e.g.* to ensure adequate sewerage and water supply for new developments and thus avoid subsequent intervention under the Public Health Acts).

Relevance to the development to be permitted

24. Unless a condition fairly and reasonably relates to the development to be permitted, it will be *ultra vires*.

25. Thus it is not sufficient that a condition is related to planning objectives: it must also be justified by the nature of the development permitted or its effect on the surroundings. For example, if planning permission is being granted for the alteration of a factory building, it would be wrong to impose conditions requiring additional parking facilities to be provided for an existing factory simply to meet a need that already exists, and similarly wrong to require the improvement of the appearance or layout of an adjoining site simply because it is untidy or congested; despite the desirability of these objectives in planning terms, the need for the action would not be created by the new development. Nevertheless it is proper for conditions to secure satisfactory access, for example, or parking facilities, genuinely required by the users of the proposed development. Conditions can also be proper where the need for them arises out of the effects of the development rather than its own features; where a permission will result in intensification of industrial use of a site, for instance, a condition may be necessary requiring additional sound-insulation in the existing factory buildings. It may even be justifiable to require by condition that an

existing building be demolished—perhaps where to have both would result in the site being over-intensively developed.

Ability to enforce

26.   A condition should not be imposed if it cannot be enforced. It is often useful to consider what means are available to secure compliance with a proposed condition. There are two provisions which authorities may use to enforce conditions: an enforcement notice, under section 172 of the Act, or a breach of condition notice under section 187A (Detailed advice about breach of condition notices is in Annex 2 of DOE Circular 17/92 (WO Circular 38/92)). Precision in the wording of conditions will be vital when it comes to enforcement (see paragraph 27 below).

Practicality of enforcement
27.   Sometimes a condition will be unenforceable because it is in practice impossible to detect a contravention. More commonly it will merely be difficult to prove a breach of its requirements. For example, a condition imposed for traffic reasons restricting the number of persons resident at any one time in a block of flats would be impracticable to monitor, and pose severe difficulties in proving a contravention. However, where a condition is intended to prevent harm to the amenities of an area which is clearly likely to result from the development (for example, a condition requiring an amusement centre to close at a certain time in the evening), it will not usually be difficult to monitor, as those affected by contravention of its requirements are likely to be able to provide clear evidence of any breaches.

Whether compliance is reasonable
28.   A condition may raise doubt about whether the person carrying out the development to which it relates can reasonably be expected to comply with it. If not, subsequent enforcement action is likely to fail on the ground that what is required cannot reasonably be enforced. One type of case where this might happen is where a condition is imposed requiring the carrying out of works (*e.g.* construction of means of access) on land within the application site but not, at the time of the grant of planning permission, under the control of the applicant. If the applicant failed to acquire an interest in that land, and carried out the development without complying with the conditions, the local planning authority could enforce the condition only by taking action against the third party who owned the land to which the condition applied, and who had gained no benefit from the development. Such difficulties can usually be avoided by framing the condition so as to require that the development authorised by the permission should not commence until the access has been constructed.

Enforcing conditions imposed on permission for operational development

29. An otherwise legally sound condition may prove unenforceable because it is imposed on a grant of planning permission for the carrying out of operations which have not been carried out in accordance with the approved plans. Authorities should take into account the Court of Appeal's judgment in the case of *Handoll and Others* v *Warner Goodman and Streat (A firm) and Others*, (1995) 25 EG 157, which held that the judgment of the Divisional Court in *Kerrier DC* v *Secretary of State for the Environment and Brewer* (1980) 41 P&CR 284, had been wrongly decided. Both cases concerned a planning permission for the erection of a dwelling subject to an agricultural occupancy condition.[3]

Test of precision

30. The framing of conditions requires care, not least to ensure that a condition is enforceable. A condition, for example, requiring only that "a landscape scheme shall be submitted for the approval of the local planning authority" is incomplete, since if the applicant were to submit the scheme, even if it is approved, the local planning authority is unlikely to be able to require the scheme to be implemented. In such a case the requirement that needs to be imposed is that landscape work shall be carried out in accordance with a scheme to be approved in writing by the local planning authority; and the wording of the condition must clearly require this. A condition of this kind also sets no requirement as to the time or the stage of development by which the landscape work must be done, which can similarly lead to enforcement difficulties. Conditions which require specific works to be carried out should state clearly when this must be done.

Vague conditions

31. A condition which is not sufficiently precise for the applicant to be able to ascertain what must be done to comply with it is *ultra vires* and cannot be imposed. Vague expressions which sometimes appear in conditions, for example such as 'keep the buildings in a tidy state', or 'so as not to cause annoyance to nearby residents', give occupants little idea of what is expected of them.

---

[3]The apparent consequences of the Court of Appeal's judgment in the *Handoll* case are that
(1) where operational development is carried out in a way which differs materially from approved plans, it amounts to development without planning permission; and
(2) any conditions imposed on the planning permission for those operations are unenforceable because the particular planning permission has not been implemented.
Authorities should ensure, in any case where planning permission has been granted for the carrying-out of operations subject to conditions, that the operations do not differ materially from the approved plans. If there is a material difference, they will need to consider seeking a specific application for planning permission to authorise the operations and granting the permission within four years of the substantial completion of those operations. They could then impose the same conditions on that permission. Alternatively, they may wish to consider taking enforcement action to remedy the breach, or to require the development to comply with the terms of the permission, if they intend to enforce the conditions.

Conditions should not be made subject to qualifications such as 'if called upon to do so', or 'if the growth of traffic makes it desirable', which do not provide any objective and certain criteria by which the applicant can ascertain what is required.

Discretionary or vetting conditions

32. Conditions which attempt to provide for an arbiter to interpret such expressions or qualifications do not avoid this difficulty. Conditions requiring that tidiness, for example, shall be 'to the satisfaction of the local planning authority' make the applicant no more certain of just what is required. Conditions which are imprecise or unreasonable cannot be made acceptable by phrases such as "except with the prior approval of the local planning authority" which purport to provide an informal procedure to waive or modify their effect. Similarly, conditions restricting the occupation of a building should not set up a vetting procedure for prospective occupiers. Conditions which raise these difficulties, however, are not to be confused with conditions which require the submission of a scheme or details for approval which will, when granted, provide the precise guidelines to be followed by the developer (see paragraph 47 below). Nor should they be confused with occupancy conditions which follow the specific criteria on affordable housing included in a development plan, if these are imposed to ensure that the housing provided is used as intended, where a different planning decision might have been taken if the proposed development did not provide for affordable housing.

Clarity

33. Conditions should be not only precise but also clear. Where a precise condition may be difficult to follow, it may be helpful to attach to the permission an illustrative plan (*e.g.* describing sight lines required at the entrance to an access road).

Reasonableness

34. A condition can be *ultra vires* on the grounds of unreasonableness, even though it may be precisely worded and apparently within the powers available.

Conditions invalid on ground of unreasonableness

35. A condition may be unreasonable because it is unduly restrictive. Although a condition may in principle impose a continuing restriction on that use of land (provided that there are good planning reasons for that restriction), such a condition should not be imposed if the restriction effectively nullifies the benefit of the permission. For example, it would normally be reasonable to restrict the hours during which an industrial use may be carried on if the use of the premises outside these hours would affect the amenities of the neighbourhood, but it would be unreasonable to do so to such an extent as to make it impossible

for the occupier to run the business properly. If it appears that a permission could be given only subject to conditions that would be likely to be held unreasonable by the courts then it will be necessary to refuse permission altogether.

Avoidance of onerous requirements

36. Even where a condition would not be so unreasonably restrictive as to be *ultra vires*, it may still be so onerous that as a matter of policy it should be avoided. Any condition which would put a severe limitation on the freedom of owners to dispose of their property, or which would obviously make it difficult to finance the erection of the permitted building by borrowing on mortgage, should be avoided on these grounds. An unduly restrictive condition can never be made acceptable by offering the prospect of informal relaxation of its effect (see paragraph 32 above).

Control over land

37. Particular care needs to be taken over conditions which require works to be carried out on land in which the applicant has no interest at the time when planning permission is granted. If the land is included in the site in respect of which the application is made, such conditions can in principle be imposed, but the authority should have regard to the points discussed in paragraph 28 above. If the land is outside that site, a condition requiring the carrying out of works on the land cannot be imposed unless the authority are satisfied that the applicant has sufficient control over the land to enable those works to be carried out (see, however, paragraphs 38-41 below).

Conditions depending on others' actions

38. It is unreasonable to impose a condition worded in a positive form which developers would be unable to comply with themselves, or which they could comply with only with the consent or authorisation of a third part (for example, a condition which requires an aerodrome owner to impose a particular pattern of aircraft flight routeings, where air traffic services for the particular aerodrome are the responsibility of the Civil Aviation Authority or the National Air Traffic Service). Similarly, conditions which require the applicant to obtain an authorisation from another body (such as Her Majesty's Inspectorate of Pollution) should not be imposed.

39. Although it would be *ultra vires*, however, to require works which the developer has not power to carry out, or which would need the consent or authorisation of a third party, it may be possible to achieve a similar result by a condition worded in negative form, prohibiting development until a specified action has been taken.

40. It is the policy of the Secretaries of State that such a condition should only be imposed on a planning permission if there are at least reasonable prospects

of the action in question being performed within the time-limit imposed by the permission.[4]

41. Thus for example, if it could be shown that, although current sewerage facilities were inadequate for a new housing estate, improvements were under way and that there are reasonable prospects that the facilities would be completed not long after the houses, it might be appropriate to grant permission subject to a condition that the houses should not be occupied until the relevant sewerage works were complete. In an appropriate case, too, it might be reasonable to use a condition requiring that the development should not commence until a particular highway had been stopped up or diverted, if there were reasonable prospects that the highway authority would be able and willing to take the necessary action.

Consent of applicant to unreasonable conditions

42. An unreasonable condition does not become reasonable because an applicant suggests it or consents to its terms. The condition will normally run with the land, and may therefore still be operative long after the applicant has moved on; it must always be justified on its planning merits.

Regulation of development

Outline permissions

43. An applicant who proposes to carry out building operations may choose to apply either for full planning permission, or for outline permission with one or more of the following matters reserved by condition for the subsequent approval of the local planning authority: the siting of the building, its design, its external appearance, the means of access, or the landscaping of the site ("reserved matters") (*cf* model condition 2). An applicant cannot seek an outline planning permission for a change of use alone or for operations other than building operations.

Details supplied in outline applications

44. An applicant can however choose to submit as part of an outline application details of any of these "reserved matters". Unless the applicant has indicated that those details are submitted "for illustrative purposes only" (or has otherwise indicated that they are not formally part of the application), the local planning authority must treat them as part of the development in respect of

---

[4]*British Railways Board* v *Secretary of State for the Environment and Hounslow LBC* [1994] JPL 32; [1993] 3 PLR 125—the House of Lords established that the mere fact that a desirable condition, worded in a negative form, appears to have no reasonable prospects of fulfilment does not mean that planning permission must necessarily be refused as a matter of law. However, the judgment leaves open the possibility for the Secretary of State, to maintain as a matter of policy that there should be at least reasonable prospects of the action in question being performed within the time-limit imposed by the permission.

which the application is being made; the authority cannot reserve that matter by condition for subsequent approval, unless the applicant is willing to amend the application by withdrawing the details.

Conditions relating to outline permissions

45. Once outline planning permission has been granted, it cannot be withdrawn except by a revocation order under section 97 of the Act, and any subsequent approval of reserved matters does not constitute the granting of a further planning permission. Any conditions relating to anything other than the reserved matters should be imposed when outline permission is granted. The only conditions which can be imposed when the reserved matters are approved are conditions which directly relate to those matters. So, where certain aspects of the development are crucial to the decision, local planning authorities will wish to consider imposing relevant conditions when outline permission is granted. For example, it may be considered necessary to require a building to be constructed within a specified "footprint" or to retain important landscape features which would affect the setting of the building and its neighbours.

46. If the local planning authority consider that whatever the precise form the development is to take, access to the buildings should be from a particular road (or, alternatively, that there should be no means of access from a particular road), then a condition to this effect must be imposed on the outline permission. Approval of the details of the means of access to the permitted buildings can be refused on the grounds that there should not be access to the site from a particular road only if the need for such a restriction arises from the details of the development which have been submitted for approval (e.g. from the density which is indicated by submitted details of the design and siting of the buildings). It is desirable that, wherever possible, notes should be appended to an outline permission to give the developer guidance as to what precise form of development will be acceptable to the local planning authority.

Conditions reserving other matters

47. Authorities should seek to ensure, where possible, that conditions other than those relating to reserved matters are self-contained, and do not require further approvals to be obtained before development can begin. Where necessary, however, a local planning authority may also when granting a full or outline planning permission, impose a condition requiring that details of a specified aspect of the development which was not fully described in the application (e.g. the provision of car parking spaces) be submitted for approval before the development is begun (cf model condition 20). In the case of a full permission, such a condition can relate to details (such as landscape works) which might have been reserved matters had the application been made in outline. The applicant has the same right of appeal to the Secretary of State under section 78 of the Act if they (sic) cannot get the authority's approval,

agreement or consent to matters reserved under such a condition as they have in respect of applications for approval of reserved matters.

Design and landscape

48. The appearance of a proposed development and its relationship to its surroundings are material considerations. As explained in Annex A to PPG1: General Policy and Principles, local authorities should not attempt to use conditions simply to impose matters of taste on applicants for planning permission. But, there will, however, be circumstances where it is important to secure a high quality of design in a proposal if this is to make a positive contribution to a site and its surroundings and show consideration for its local context. In such cases, the use of conditions may be acceptable. The appearance and treatment of the spaces between and around buildings is also of great importance. Similarly, local planning authorities may wish to use conditions to ensure that important vistas are preserved or that landscape features are provided to improve the overall setting of a development.

49. Landscape design may raise special considerations. The treatment of open space can vary greatly and the objective should be to ensure that the intended design quality is achieved in practice. It is therefore especially important for the authority to give some advance indication of the essential characteristics of an acceptable landscape scheme—always bearing in mind that such requirements should not be unreasonable. It is of equal importance to ensure that the design proposals are reflected in the quality of works and materials that result in the final product. The design and implementation stages of landscape treatment may therefore be addressed more successfully by separate conditions, occurring as they do at different stages and under differing circumstances. The visual impact of a development will often need to be assessed as a whole, and this may well involve considering details of landscape design together with other reserved matters.

Enforcement of landscape requirements

50. To ensure that a landscape design scheme is prepared, conditions may require that no development should take place until the scheme is approved, so long as this requirement is reasonable (model condition 25). Enforcing compliance with landscape schemes can pose problems, since work on landscaping can rarely proceed until building operations are nearing completion, and only on permissions for a change of use would it be acceptable to provide that the development permitted should not proceed until the landscape work had been substantially completed. Where permission is being granted for a substantial estate of houses, it might be thought appropriate to frame the relevant condition to allow for landscape works to be phased in accordance with a programme or timetable to be agreed between the developer and the authority and submitted for approval as part of the landscape design

proposals. Alternatively, the erection of the last few houses might be prohibited until planting has been completed in accordance with the landscape scheme; but in relation to a permission for an industrial or office building it would be possible to impose a condition prohibiting or restricting occupation of the building until such words have been completed.

Trees

51. Section 197 of the Act places an express duty on the local planning authority, when granting planning permission, to ensure whenever appropriate that adequate conditions are imposed to secure the preservation or planting of trees, and that any necessary tree preservation orders are made under section 198 of the Act. When granting outline planning permission, the authority may consider it appropriate to impose a condition requiring the submission of particular details relating to trees to be retained on the site, such as their location in relation to the proposed development and their general state of health and stability. When granting detailed planning permission, conditions may be used to secure the protection of trees to be retained, for example by requiring the erection of fencing around trees during the course of development or restricting works which are likely to adversely affect them. The long-term protection of trees, however, should be secured by tree preservation orders rather than by condition; such orders may also be expedient for the temporary protection of existing trees until details of the reserved matters are submitted and it becomes clear whether there is a need to retain the trees.

52. The planting and establishment of new trees may need work over several months or years, and the authority may wish to ensure that they secure details of those responsible for the management and maintenance of certain planted areas during that period of time. Where appropriate, a condition may require not just initial planting, but also that trees shall be maintained during the first few years (specifying the number of years) and that any which die or are removed within that time shall be replaced. DOE Circular 36/78 (WO 64/78) deals in more detail with the use of conditions in relation to trees and with trees and development generally. See also model conditions 71-75 Appendix 4 of DOE Circular 36/78 (WO 64/78) is hereby cancelled.

Time-limits on the commencement of development

Statutory time-limits
53. The imposition of time-limits on the commencement of development is not required by the Act for temporary permissions (paragraphs 108-113 below), or for permissions granted by a development order or an enterprise zone scheme.

Time-limits on full permissions

54. Other grants of planning permission (apart from outline permissions) must, under section 91 of the Act, be made subject to a condition imposing a time-limit within which the development authorised must be started. The section specifies a period of five years from the date of the permission (model condition 1) (but see paragraph 55 below). Where planning permission is granted without a condition limiting the duration of the planning permission, it is deemed to be granted subject to the condition that the development to which it relates must be begun not later than the expiration of 5 years beginning with the grant of permission.

Time-limits on outline permissions

55. Grants of outline planning permission must, under section 92 of the Act, be made subject to conditions imposing two types of time-limit, one within which applications must be made for the approval of reserved matters and a second within which the development itself must be started (model conditions 4 and 5). The periods specified in the section are three years from the grant of outline permission for the submission of applications for approval of reserved matters, and either five years from the grant of permission, or two years from the final approval of the last of the reserved matters, whichever is the longer, for starting the development.

Variation from standard time-limits

56. If the authority consider it appropriate on planning grounds, however, they may use longer or shorter periods than those specified in the Act, and must give their reasons for so doing. In the absence of specific time-limiting conditions, permission is deemed to have been granted subject to conditions imposing the periods referred to in paragraphs 54 and 55 above. It may be particularly desirable to adopt a flexible approach to the fixing of time-limits where development is to be carried out in distinct parts or phases; section 92(5) of the Act provides that outline permissions may be granted subject to a series of time-limits, each relating to a separate part of the development. Such a condition must be imposed at the time outline planning permission is granted.

Separate submission of different reserved matters

57. Applications for approval under an outline permission may be made either for all reserved matters at once, or for one at one time and others at another. Even after details relating to a particular reserved matter have been approved, one or more fresh applications may be made for approval of alternative details in relation to the same reserved matter. Once the time-limit for applications for approval of reserved matters has expired, however, no applications for such an approval can be made.

58. A condition requiring the developer to obtain approval of reserved matters within a stated period should not be used, since the timing of an approval is not

within the developer's control. A condition, therefore, should set time-limits only on the submission of reserved matters.

Effect of time-limit

59. After the expiry of the time-limit for commencement of development it is not possible for development to be begun under that permission; a further application for planning permission must be made (see paragraph 4 above).

Renewal of permissions before expiry of time-limits

60. Developers who delay the start of development are likely, as the time-limit for implementation approaches, to want their permission renewed. Under Regulation 3 of the Town and Country Planning (Applications) Regulations 1988, applications for such renewals may be made simply by letter, referring to the existing planning permission, although the local planning authority have power subsequently to require further information if needed. As a general rule, such applications should be refused only where:

(a) there has been some material change in planning circumstances since the original permission was granted (*e.g.* a change in some relevant planning policy for the area, or in relevant highway considerations, or the publication by the Government of new planning policy guidance, material to the renewal application);

(b) continued failure to begin the development will contribute unacceptably to uncertainty about the future pattern of development in the area; or

(c) the application is premature because the permission still has a reasonable time to run.

Completion of development

Completion of whole of development

61. A condition requiring that the whole of the development permitted be completed is likely to be difficult to enforce. If a development forming a single indivisible whole, such as a single dwellinghouse, is left half-finished it may be possible to secure completion by means of a completion notice under section 94 of the Act. If, however, the reason for failure to complete, is financial difficulties experienced by the developer, neither a completion notice nor the enforcement of conditions would be likely to succeed; in such circumstances it may be that the only practical step open to the local planning authority, if they wish to secure the completion of the development, is the acquisition of the land. If a large development such as an estate of houses is left half-complete, this may well be because of market changes (for example, a shift of demand from four-bedroom to two-bedroom houses), and it would clearly not be desirable to compel the erection of houses of a type for which there was no demand or need.

Conditions requiring the completion of the whole of a development should therefore not normally be imposed.

Completion of elements of a development

62. Conditions may be needed, however, to secure that a particular element in a scheme is provided by a particular stage or before the scheme is brought into use, or to secure the provision of an element of a kind a developer might otherwise be inclined to defer or omit. Thus it may be desirable to require that a new access to the site should be constructed before any other development is carried out; or, where an office scheme includes a car park, that the car park is completed before the offices are occupied; or, where the scheme includes both offices and housing, that the offices should not be occupied before the houses are complete. The approach adopted must, of course, be reasonable. Taking the last example, it could well be unacceptable to require that the houses should be completed before the offices are begun: this would be likely to be an unjustifiable interference with the way the development is carried out. Or, to take another example, it could well be unacceptable to demand that all the requirements of a landscape condition should be complied with before a building is occupied; this could involve the building lying empty for many months, since such a condition will often provide for a considerable maintenance period so that trees may become established (on landscape design, see paragraphs 48-50 above).

Phasing

Phasing required by infrastructure

63. Conditions may also be imposed to ensure that development proceeds in a certain sequence where some circumstance of the case (*e.g.* the manner of provision of infrastructure) makes this necessary. See model condition 42.

Highway conditions

Parking, public transport, walking and cycling

64. Developments often generate extra traffic, usually in the form of haulage or delivery vehicles or cars belonging to residents, visitors or employees. Unless this demand is minimal (as it might be, for example, in the case of some very small firms), and unlikely to cause obstruction, space may need to be provided to allow for parking.

65. Any conditions specifying the number of parking spaces should support the locational policies in the development plan, but they also need to be reasonable in relation to the size and nature of the development and to satisfy the other tests in paragraph 14 above.

66. Sometimes parking space in the form of a lay-by will be satisfactory. More often a parking site separate from the highway will be needed. In the latter case, conditions should ensure, where necessary, that space is provided for the turning of vehicles so that they do not have to reverse on to the highway.

67. Where the authority decides that it is appropriate to require the provision of car parking spaces on other land under the control of the applicant, the development must be readily accessible from the car park.

68. In certain circumstances, developers may enter into a planning obligation with the local planning authority to provide off-site parking or to contribute to measures to assist public transport or walking and cycling—see paragraphs B5-B10 or DOE Circular 16/91 (WO 53/91) and PPG13: Transport (but not for Wales where the former version of PPG13 [November 1988] continues to apply). Advice on how local authorities should integrate transport and land use planning is also contained in PPG13.

Access

69. Where a service road is needed as part of a large development for which outline permission is to be granted, it may be necessary to impose a condition requiring all access to the highway to be by means of the service road. If such a condition is not imposed at outline stage it may not be possible to secure the objective at a later stage (see paragraph 45). Similarly, if it is desired that there should be no direct access on to a main road, or that access must be taken from a particular side road, a condition to that effect should be imposed on the outline permission, as without such a condition these restrictions could not normally be made at the stage of consideration of details.

70. A condition may require the provision or improvement of a service road or means of access even if such works are not included in the application, provided that they can be undertaken on the site in respect of which the application is made, or on other land which is under the control of the applicant and sufficiently relates to the proposed development. The condition should be framed so as to require the laying out or improvement of the means of access, or the relevant section of the service road, on defined land before the relevant buildings are occupied. (Policy advice and guidance about conditions requiring works in the highway is contained in Annex C to PPG13: Transport (but not for Wales where the former version of PPG13 [November 1988] continues to apply)).

Lorry routeing

71. Planning conditions are not an appropriate means of controlling the right of passage over public highways. Although negatively worded conditions which control such matters might sometimes be capable of being validly imposed on planning permissions, such conditions are likely to be very difficult to enforce effectively. It may be possible to encourage drivers to follow preferred routes by

posting site notices to that effect, or by requiring them to use a particular entrance to (or exit from) the site. But where it is essential to prevent traffic from using particular routes, the correct mechanism for doing so is an Order under either section 1 or section 6 (as appropriate) of the Road Traffic Regulation Act 1984.

Cession of land

72. Conditions may not require the cession of land to other parties, such as the highway authority.

Development of contaminated sites

Contaminated land

73. Land formerly used for industrial purposes or for waste disposal can be contaminated by substances that pose immediate or long-term hazards to the environment or to health, or which may damage any buildings erected on such sites. Contaminants may also escape from the site to cause air and water pollution and pollution of nearby land; the emission of landfill gas may be particularly hazardous. In these circumstances, appropriate conditions may be imposed in order to ensure that the development proposed for the site will not expose future users or occupiers of the site, any buildings and services, or the wider environment to risks associated with the contaminants present. However, local planning authorities should base any such conditions on a site-specific assessment of the environmental risks which might affect, or be affected by, the particular proposed development.

74. If it is known or strongly suspected that a site is contaminated to an extent which would adversely affect the proposed development or infringe statutory requirements, an investigation of the hazards by the developer and proposals for remedial action will normally be required before the application can be determined by the planning authority. Any subsequent planning permission may need to include planning conditions requiring certain remedial measures to be carried out.

75. In cases where there is only a suspicion that the site might be contaminated, or where the evidence suggests that there may be only slight contamination, planning permission may be granted subject to conditions that development will not be permitted to start until a site investigation and assessment have been carried out an that the development itself will incorporate any remedial measures shown to be necessary.

76. Conditions might also be imposed requiring the developer to draw to the attention of the planning authority the presence of significant unsuspected contamination encountered during redevelopment. Further planning policy

guidance on contaminated land is contained in PPG23: Planning and Pollution Control (England only) (paragraph 4 and Annex 10) (in Wales, Welsh Office Circular 22/87—Contaminated land. (See also model conditions 56-58).

Environmental assessment

77. For projects subject to environmental assessment, conditions attached to a grant of planning permission may incorporate mitigation measures proposed in an environmental statement where such conditions meet the criteria summarised in paragraph 14 above. It may be appropriate, within the powers to impose conditions on the grant of planning permission and in the light of the environmental assessment, to require a scheme of mitigation covering matters of planning concern to be submitted to and approved in writing by the local planning authority before any development is undertaken.(Model condition 25 is an example of this type of condition). Such conditions should not duplicate the effect of other legislative controls, where such controls are available. In particular, planning authorities should not seek to substitute their own judgement on pollution control issues for that of the bodies with the relevant expertise and the statutory responsibility for that control (see paragraph 1.34 of PPG23 (England only)).

Noise

78. Noise can have a significant effect on the environment and on the quality of life enjoyed by individuals and communities. The planning system should ensure that, wherever practicable, noise-sensitive developments are separated from major sources of noise, and that new development involving noisy activities should, if possible, be sited away from noise-sensitive land uses. Where it is not possible to achieve such a separation of land uses, local planning authorities should consider whether it is practicable to control or reduce noise levels, or to mitigate the impact of noise, through the use of conditions or planning obligations. Further advice is contained in PPG24: Planning and Noise (England only), and MPG11: The Control of Noise at Surface Mineral Workings. (See also model conditions 6-11).

Listed buildings

79. Guidance on conditions and listed buildings is contained in Annex B to PPG15: Planning and the Historic Environment (England only), which also contains advice about World Heritage sites (paragraphs 2.22-2.23 and 6.35-6.37).

Sites of archaeological interest

80. Scheduled ancient monuments are protected by Part I of the Ancient Monuments and Archaeological Areas Act 1979, and investigation for archaeological purposes is provided for in designated areas by Part II of that Act. Where these provisions apply, their effect should not be duplicated by planning conditions (*cf* paragraphs 21-23 above), although authorities granting planning permission in such circumstances are advised to draw the attention of the applicant to the relevant provisions of the 1979 Act.

81. Where, however, planning permission is being granted for development which might affect a monument which has not been scheduled, or which might affect land in an area which is considered to be of archaeological interest but which has not been formally designated as such under section 33 of the 1979 Act, the local planning authority may wish to impose conditions designed to protect the monument or ensure that reasonable access is given to a nominated archaeologist—either to hold a "watching brief" during the construction period or specifically to carry out archaeological investigation and recording before or in the course of the permitted operations on the site. (For further advice on archaeology and planning conditions see paragraphs 29 and 30 of PPG16: Archaeology and Planning or PPG16 (Wales), and model conditions 53-55).

Maintenance conditions

82. A condition may be imposed, where appropriate, requiring some feature of development to be retained—car parking spaces, for example, or an area of open space in a housing scheme (a better solution, however, is that adopted in model conditions 22 and 24). A condition requiring something to be maintained, in the sense of being kept in good repair or in a prescribed manner, should be imposed only when the local planning authority are fully satisfied that the requirement is both relevant to the development which is being permitted, reasonable in its effects, and sufficiently precise in its terms to be readily enforceable. Maintenance conditions should not normally be imposed when granting permission for the erection of buildings, or for works other than works of a continuing nature such as minerals extraction.

Conditions requiring a consideration for the grant of permission

83. No payment of money or other consideration can be required when granting a permission or any other kind of consent required by a statute, except where there is specific statutory authority. Conditions requiring, for instance, the cession of land for road improvements or for open space, or requiring the

developer to contribute money towards the provision of public car parking facilities, should accordingly not be attached to planning permissions. However, conditions may in some cases reasonably be imposed to oblige developers to carry out works on land within the application site, to overcome planning objections to the development *e.g.* provision of an access road. Further advice on this and on agreements with developers to cover such matters is given in "Planning Obligations" (DOE Circular 16/91, WO 53/91).

Conditions altering the nature of the development

Modifying proposed development

84. If some feature of a proposed development, or the lack of it, is unacceptable in planning terms, the best course will often be for the applicant to be invited to modify the application (if the modification is substantial, of course, a fresh application will be needed). It may however, depending on the case, be quicker and easier for the local planning authority to impose a condition modifying in some way the development permitted. The precise course of action will normally emerge during discussion with the applicant. A condition modifying the development, however, cannot be imposed if it would make the development permitted substantially different from that comprised in the application. It would thus be legitimate to require by condition that a factory proposal, for example, should include necessary car parking facilities, but wrong to grant permission for a development consisting of houses and shops subject to a condition that houses be substituted for the shops. Whether a modification would amount to substantial difference will depend upon the circumstances of the case, but a useful test will be whether it would so change the proposal that those interested in it would wish to comment on the modification.

Regulation after development

85. Conditions which will remain in force after the development has been carried out always need particular care. They can place onerous and permanent restrictions on what can be done with the premises affected, and they should therefore not be imposed without scrupulous weighing of the balance of advantage. The following paragraphs give more detailed guidance.

Conditions restricting permitted development or otherwise restricting use

Restrictions on use or permitted development

86. It is possible, exceptionally, to impose conditions to restrict further development which would normally be permitted by a development order, or to

restrict changes of use which would not be regarded as development (whether because the change is not a "material" change within the terms of section 55(1) of the Act, or by reason of section 55(2) and the provisions of the Town and Country Planning (Use Classes) Order 1987) (SI 1987/764). Changes of use can be restricted either by prohibiting any change from the use permitted or by precluding specific alternative uses (see model conditions 48-49). It should be noted, however, that a condition restricting changes of use will not restrict ancillary or incidental activities unless it so specifies (see paragraph 91 below). Similarly, a general condition which restricts the use of land does not remove permitted development rights for that use unless the condition specifically removes those rights as well.

Presumption against such restrictions

87. Both development orders and the Use Classes Order, however, are designed to give or confirm a freedom from detailed control which will be acceptable in the great majority of cases. Save in exceptional circumstances, conditions should not be imposed which restrict either permitted development rights granted by development orders or future changes of use which the Use Classes Order would otherwise allow. The Secretaries of State would regard such conditions as unreasonable unless there were clear evidence that the uses excluded would have serious adverse effects on amenity or the environment, that there were no other forms of control, and that the condition would serve a clear planning purpose.

88. It might, for example, be possible to justify imposing a condition restricting permitted development rights allowed by Part 2, Class A, of Schedule 2 to the Town and Country Planning (General Permitted Development) Order 1995 so as to preserve an exceptionally attractive open plan estate free of fences, or under Part 1, Class A of the General Permitted Development Order so as to avoid overdevelopment by extensions to dwellinghouses in an area of housing at unusually high density; or restricting changes of use so as to prevent the use of large retail premises as a food or convenience goods supermarket where such a use might generate an unacceptable level of additional traffic or have a damaging effect on the vitality of a nearby town centre; or so as to limit the storage of hazardous substances in a warehouse.

Specific conditions better than general ones

89. Because of the general presumption against such restrictions on permitted development or on changes of use which are not development, it will always be necessary to look carefully at the planning reasons for any restriction, and to ensure that the condition imposed is no more onerous than can be justified (it may be helpful to refer to paragraph 36 above). It would not be right to use a condition restricting uses where an alternative, more specific, condition would achieve the same end (for example, where it is necessary to restrict the volume of noise emitted from an industrial site, and a condition addressing the problem

expressly can be used—see model conditions 6-11—that condition should be imposed, rather than one restricting the permitted uses). Scrupulous care in the giving of proper, adequate and intelligible reasons fro imposing conditions (see paragraph 10 above) can help authorities to ensure that the conditions they impose are not more onerous than is necessary to achieve their objective.

90.   It will be preferable if a condition designed to restrict changes of use can be drafted so as to prohibit a change to a particular unacceptable use or uses, as in model condition 49 (provided the list does not become too long), rather than in terms which prevent any change of use at all; but in many cases a condition confining the use to the use permitted may be necessary (model condition 48). In appropriate circumstances, it might be reasonable to impose a condition limiting the intensification of use of small office or industrial buildings where intensification beyond a certain point would generate traffic and/or parking problems. Conditions designed to prevent the primary use of an office building being changed to use as shops are unnecessary, as such a change would involve a material change of use amounting to development of the land and thus would require planning permission in any event.

Ancillary uses
91.   Conditions are sometimes imposed restricting ancillary or incidental activities. Conditions of this kind can be burdensome to some technologically advanced industries where there may be a need for higher than normal levels of ancillary office research or storage uses, or for short-term changes in uses, or the balance of uses, which would not normally be material changes of use involving development. Such conditions should therefore not normally be imposed on permissions for manufacturing or service industry, except where they are designed to preclude or regulate activities giving rise to hazard, noise or offensive emissions.

Conditions restricting the occupancy of buildings and land

Occupancy: general considerations
92.   Since planning controls are concerned with the use of land rather than the identity of the user, the question of who is to occupy premises for which permission is to be granted will normally be irrelevant. Conditions restricting occupancy to a particular occupier or class of occupier should only be used when special planning grounds can be demonstrated, and where the alternative would normally be refusal of permission.

Personal permissions
93.   Unless the permission otherwise provides, planning permission runs with the land and it is seldom desirable to provide otherwise. There are occasions, however, where it is proposed exceptionally to grant permission for the use of a building or land for some purpose which would not normally be allowed at the

site, simply because there are strong compassionate or other personal grounds for doing so. In such a case the permission should normally be made subject to a condition that it shall enure only for the benefit of a named person—usually the applicant (model condition 35): a permission personal to a company is inappropriate because its shares can be transferred to other persons without affecting the legal personality of the company. This condition will scarcely ever be justified in the case of a permission for the erection of a permanent building.

General undesirability of commercial and industrial occupancy conditions
94.   Conditions are sometimes imposed to confine the occupation of commercial or industrial premises to local firms. Such conditions can act—undesirably—to protect local businesses against fair competition, and may hinder the movement of industry in response to economic demand. If a service, or the employment it generates, is needed in an area, there is no planning reason why it should be provided by one firm rather than another. Commercial and industrial buildings in an area of open countryside will not become more acceptable because their occupancy is restricted, nor will the expansion of a local firm necessarily lead to less pressure for further development (*e.g.* housing) than the arrival of a firm from outside. The Secretaries of State therefore regard such conditions as undesirable in principle. (For further policy guidance see PPG4: Industrial and Commercial Development and Small Firms).

Exception where occupancy conditions may be appropriate
95.   However, where the need of a local firm to expand is sufficiently exceptional to justify a departure from a general policy of restraint it will be essential to ensure that such a permission is not abused. It may be reasonable to impose a "local occupancy" condition in such circumstances, provided it is for a limited period (10 years is considered to be a suitable maximum), covers a large catchment area (for example, the area of the relevant county) and clearly defines the categories of persons or firms who may occupy the premises. Occupancy conditions should be imposed only where special planning grounds can be demonstrated and where the alternative would normally be to refuse the application. It would not normally be appropriate to impose such conditions on small buildings of less than 300 square metres of office floorspace (or 500 square metres of industrial floorspace). Occupancy conditions should not be imposed which provide for a system of vetting by the local planning authority or the use of a vague test such as "needing to be located in the area".

Domestic occupancy conditions
96.   Subject to the advice about affordable housing (paragraph 97 below), staff accommodation (paragraphs 100-101), agricultural dwellings (paragraphs 102-105), and seasonal use (paragraphs 115-117), if the development of a site for housing is an acceptable use of the land there will seldom be any good reason on land-use planning grounds to restrict the occupancy of those houses to a

particular type of person (*e.g.* those already living or working in the area). To impose such a condition is to draw an artificial and unwarranted distinction between new houses or new conversions and existing houses that are not subject to such restrictions on occupancy or sale. It may deter housebuilders from providing homes for which there is a local demand and building societies from providing mortgage finance. It may also impose hardship on owners who subsequently need to sell. It involves too detailed and onerous an application of development control and too great an interference in the rights of individual ownership. In the view of the Secretaries of State, such conditions should therefore not be imposed save in the most exceptional cases where there are clear and specific circumstances that warrant allowing an individual house (or extension) on a site where development would not normally be permitted.

Affordable housing

97. The courts have held that the community's need for a mix of housing types—including affordable housing—is capable of being a material planning consideration. It follows that there may be circumstances in which it will be acceptable to use conditions to ensure that some of the housing built is occupied only by people falling within particular categories of need. Such conditions would normally only be necessary where a different planning decision might have been taken if the proposed development did not provide for affordable housing and should make clear the nature of the restriction by referring to criteria set out in the relevant local plan policy. Conditions should not normally be used to control matters such as tenure, price or ownership. More detailed advice on affordable housing is contained in PPG3: Housing (PPG3 (Wales): Land for Housing in Wales).

"Granny"/Staff Annexes

98. Some extensions to dwellings are intended for use as "granny annexes". It is possible that a "granny annex" which provides independent living accommodation, could subsequently be let or sold off separately from the main dwelling. Where there are sound planning reasons why the creation of an additional dwelling would be unacceptable it may be appropriate, to impose a planning condition to the effect that the extension permitted shall be used solely as accommodation ancillary to the main dwelling house. See model condition 47.

99. The same is true for separate buildings (often conversions of outbuildings) intended for use as "granny annexes". In these cases it is even more likely that a separate unit of accommodation will be created.

Staff accommodation

100. The above considerations may equally apply to staff accommodation. Where an existing house is within the curtilage of another building, and the two are in the same occupation, any proposal to occupy the two buildings separately

is likely to amount to a material change of use, so that planning permission would be required for such a proposal even in the absence of a condition. Local planning authorities should normally consider applications for such development sympathetically, since if the need for such a dwelling for the accommodation of an employee, for example, disappears, there will generally be no justification for requiring the building to stand empty or to be demolished.

101. Conditions tying the occupation of dwellings to that of separate buildings (*e.g.* requiring a house to be occupied only by a person employed by a nearby garage) should be avoided. However, exceptionally, such conditions may be appropriate where there are sound planning reasons to justify them *e.g.* where a dwelling has been allowed on a site where permission would not normally be granted. To grant an unconditional permission would mean that the dwelling could be sold off for general use thereby undermining established countryside policy. To ensure that the dwelling remains available to meet the identified need it may therefore be acceptable to grant permission subject to a condition that ties the occupation of the new house to the existing business. (See model condition 46.)

Agricultural dwellings

102. Despite planning policies which impose strict controls on new residential development in the open countryside, there may be circumstances where permission is granted to allow a house to be built to accommodate an agricultural or forestry worker on a site where residential development would not normally be permitted. In these circumstances, a condition should be imposed to ensure that the dwellings are kept available for meeting this need— see model condition 45.[5]

103. It should not be necessary to tie occupation of the dwelling to workers engaged in one specific farm or forestry business even though the needs of that business justified the provision of the dwelling. The model occupancy condition will ensure that the dwelling is kept available to meet the needs of other farm or forestry businesses in the locality if it is no longer needed by the original business, thus avoiding a proliferation of dwellings in the open countryside (see Annex E of PPG7: The Countryside and the Rural Economy for further details about agricultural and forestry dwellings).

104. Local planning authorities will wish to take care to frame agricultural occupancy condition s in such a way as to ensure that their purpose is clear. In

[5]Model condition 45 includes the words "... limited to a person solely or mainly working, or last working, in the locality in agriculture or forestry ...". "Last working" covers the case both of a person who is temporarily unemployed or of a person who from old age, or illness, is no longer able to work. Nor need the words necessarily exclude a person who is engaged in other part-time, or temporary employment, if that person could still be regarded as a farm worker or retired farm worker, or a worker in one of the other specified categories. (*Fawcett Properties Ltd v Buckingham County Council* [1961] AC 636 at pages 671 to 672).
A person who last worked in agriculture/forestry but who now works on a permanent basis mainly in non-agricultural/forestry employment, would *not* satisfy model condition 45.

particular, they will wish to ensure that the condition does not have the effect of preventing occupation by the dependants of the person defined (the agricultural occupant).[6]

105. Where an agricultural occupancy condition has been imposed it will not be appropriate to remove it on a subsequent application unless it is shown that the existing need for dwellings for agricultural workers in the locality no longer warrants reserving the house for that purpose. This assessment will be necessary in all cases, including those where the condition was originally inappropriately imposed (*Sevenoaks DC v Secretary of State for the Environment and Mr and Mrs Geer* (1995)69 P.&C.R.87). However, the fact that planning permission for a dwelling would in all probability be granted today without an agricultural occupancy condition is a material consideration (*Hambleton DC v Secretary of State for the Environment and others* [1994] EGCS 202).

Conditions governing size of unit occupied

106. Conditions requiring that a large commercial or industrial building should be occupied either only as a single unit, or alternatively only in suites not exceeding a certain area of floorspace, represent, in the view of the Secretaries of State, a significant interference with property rights which is likely to inhibit or delay the productive use of the buildings affected. Such conditions therefore should normally be avoided unless there are sound planning reasons to impose them. For example, in the case of retail development, it may be appropriate to impose conditions to control the number or size of units to prevent the development being subdivided into a large number of outlets (or vice versa), if the effect of such a change would be to change significantly the nature of the retail development to one that would not have been given permission, or would increase the need for parking or alter significantly the traffic and transport impact of the proposal.

Retail development

107. Retail parks can change their composition over time. If such a change would create a development that the planning authority would have refused on the grounds of impact on vitality and viability of an existing town centre, it may be sensible to consider the use of planning conditions to ensure that these developments do not subsequently change their character unacceptably. Any conditions imposed should apply only to the main ranges of goods (*e.g.* food and convenience goods, hardware, electrical goods, furniture and carpets) and should not seek to control details of particular products to be sold. For further advice see PPG6: Town Centres and Retail Development.

[6]"Dependants" means persons living in family with the person defined and dependent on him (or her) in whole or in part for their subsistence and support (*Fawcett Properties Ltd v Buckingham County Council* [1961] AC 636 at page 671).

Temporary permissions

108. Section 72(1)(b) of the Act gives power to impose conditions requiring that a use be discontinued or that buildings or works be removed at the end of a specified period (where permission is granted for the development of the operational land of a statutory undertaker, however, this power does not apply except with the undertaker's consent: section 267 of the Act). Conditions of this kind are sometimes confused with conditions which impose a time-limit for the implementation of a permission (paragraphs 65-60 above), but they are quite distinct, and different considerations arise in relation to them.

Principles applying to temporary permissions

109. Advice on minerals permissions is given in Minerals Policy Guidance notes. In other cases, in deciding whether a temporary permission is appropriate, three main factors should be taken into account. First, it will rarely be necessary to give a temporary permission to an applicant who wishes to carry out development which conforms with the provisions of the development plan. Next, it is undesirable to impose a condition requiring the demolition after a stated period of a building that is clearly intended to be permanent. Lastly, the material considerations to which regard must be had in granting any permission are not limited or made different by a decision to make the permission a temporary one. Thus, the reason for granting a temporary permission can never be that a time-limit is necessary because of the effect of the development on the amenities of the area. Where such objections to a development arise they should, if necessary, be met instead by conditions whose requirements will safeguard the amenities. If it is not possible to devise such conditions, and if the damage to amenity cannot be accepted, then the only course open is to refuse permission. These considerations will mean that a temporary permission will normally only be appropriate either where the applicant proposes temporary development, or when a trial run is needed in order to assess the effect of the development on the area.

Short-term buildings or uses

110. Where a proposal relates to a building or use which the applicant is expected to retain or continue only for a limited period, whether because they have specifically volunteered that intention, or because it is expected that the planning circumstances will change in a particular way at the end of that period, then a temporary permission may be justified. For example, permission might reasonably be granted on an application for the erection of a temporary building to last seven years on land which will be required for road improvements eight or more years hence, although an application to erect a permanent building on the land would normally be refused.

Trial runs

111. Again, where an application is made for permanent permission for a use which may be "potentially detrimental" to existing uses nearby, but there is insufficient evidence to enable the authority to be sure of its character or effect, it might be appropriate to grant a temporary permission in order to give the development a trial run, provided that such a permission would be reasonable having regard to the capital expenditure necessary to carry out the development. However, a temporary permission would not be justified merely because, for example, a building is to be made of wood rather than brick. Nor would a temporary permission be justified on the grounds that, although a particular use, such as a hostel or playgroup, would be acceptable in a certain location, the character of its management may change. In certain circumstances it may be possible to grant temporary permission for the provision of a caravan or other temporary accommodation where there is some evidence to support the grant of planning permission for an application for an agricultural or forestry dwelling, but it is inconclusive, perhaps because there is doubt about the sustainability of the proposed enterprise. This allows time for such prospects to be clarified.

112. A second temporary permission should not normally be granted. A trial period should be set that is sufficiently long for it to be clear by the end of the first permission whether permanent permission or a refusal is the right answer. Usually a second temporary permission will only be justified where highway or redevelopment proposals have been postponed, or in cases of hardship where temporary instead of personal permission has been granted for a change of use.

Restoration of sites

113. If the temporary permission is for development consisting of or including the carrying out of operations, it is important to make provision by condition for the removal of any buildings and works permitted—not merely for the cessation of the use—and for the reinstatement of the land, when the permission expires (model condition 41). Where the permission is for temporary use of land as a caravan site, conditions may include a requirement to remove at the expiry of the permission any buildings or structures, such as toilet blocks, erected under Part 5 of the General Permitted Development Order.[7]

Access for disabled people

114. Where a building is new, or is being altered, it is usually sufficient to rely on building regulations to ensure adequate access for disabled people. However, some new development does not require building regulation approval *e.g.*

---

[7] This section does not deal with specific legislation or advice on restoration of mineral workings, where all permissions are time-limited; nor on restoration of landfill sites. Advice on restoration of mineral workings is in MPG7; and for landfill sites in Annex 11 of PPG23 (England only).

development affecting the setting of buildings (layout of estates, pedestrianisation etc.) rather than the buildings themselves. Where there is a clear planning need, it may be appropriate to impose a condition to ensure adequate access for disabled people. (See model condition 37.)

Seasonal use

Seasonal occupancy conditions

115. Occasionally it may be acceptable to limit the use of land for a particular purpose to certain seasons of the year. For example, where planning permission is being granted for a caravan site, the local planning authority may think it necessary to impose a condition to ensure that during the winter months the caravans are not occupied and are removed for storage to a particular part of the site or away from the site altogether; a suitable form of condition to secure seasonal use is given in model condition 43. Where such a condition is imposed, particular care should be taken to see that the condition allows a reasonable period of use of the caravans in each year. A similar approach may be taken where it is necessary to prevent the permanent residential use of holiday chalets which by the character of their construction or design are unsuitable for continuous occupation. Seasonal occupancy conditions may also be appropriate to protect the local environment, for example, where the site is near a fragile habitat which requires peace and quiet to allow seasonal breeding or winter feeding to take place.

Holiday occupancy conditions

116. In recent years there has been an increased demand for self-catering holiday accommodation —whether new buildings (including mobile homes) or converted properties—which may be constructed to a standard that would equally support permanent residence in some comfort. But this accommodation may also be located in areas in which the provision of permanent housing would be contrary to national policies on development in the countryside or not in accordance with development plan policies, or both. The Secretaries of State consider that the planning system should respond to these changes without compromising policies to safeguard the countryside.

117. There may be circumstances where it will be reasonable for the local planning authority to grant planning permission for holiday accommodation as an exception to these policies, with a condition specifying its use as holiday accommodation only. For example, conversions of redundant buildings into holiday accommodation where conversion to residential dwellings would not be permitted may reduce the pressure on other housing in rural areas. A holiday occupancy condition would seem more appropriate in those circumstances than a seasonal occupancy condition. But authorities should continue to use seasonal

occupancy conditions to prevent the permanent residential use of accommodation which by the character of its construction or design is unsuitable for continuous occupation, particularly in the winter months. (For further advice about holiday and seasonal occupancy conditions see Annex C to PPG21: Tourism)

Nature conservation

118. Nature conservation can be a significant material consideration in determining many planning applications. But local planning authorities should not refuse permission if development can be permitted subject to conditions that will prevent damaging impacts on wildlife habitats or important physical features. Where there is a risk of damage to a site, the planning authority should consider the use of conditions or planning obligations in the interests of nature conservation. Conditions can be used, for example, to require areas to be fenced or bunded off to protect them or to restrict operations or uses at particular times of the year.

119. In addition, there are certain special sites where any conditions or obligations affecting them will need to be consistent with the provisions applicable for their protection. In some cases the provisions have statutory force. For further advice see PPG9: Nature Conservation (England only).

Protected species

120. Local planning authorities should not refuse planning permission if appropriate conditions can be imposed or planning obligations entered into which are designed to prevent deliberate harm to the protected species. For further advice see paragraphs 44-48 of PPG9 (England only).

Appendix A

Suggested models of acceptable conditions for use in appropriate circumstances

Notes

> (i) No condition should be imposed unless, having regard to the circumstances of each case, it meets the tests set out in the Annex to this Circular. The conditions set out below are only models, and may

need adaptation to the circumstances of particular cases. The model conditions are formulated in relation to proposed development and will not necessarily be appropriate for retrospective applications.

(ii) This list is not exhaustive, and it will be possible to word many acceptable conditions to meet planning problems which are not mentioned here.

(iii) Model reasons for the imposition of the conditions shown below cannot be given, as the reasons for imposing conditions will vary in each case, depending on its circumstances.

(iv) Entries [thus] are words in the models which will commonly need variation, or alternative wording; entries [*thus*] are descriptions of what is to be inserted in a model: entries *thus* are explanatory notes. A reference to (*paragraph 11*) refers to paragraph 11 of the Annex to this Circular.

Time limit for commencement of development

1. The development hereby permitted shall be begun before the expiration of [five] years from the date of this permission.

In the case of full permissions (paragraph 54).

Outline permissions

2. Approval of the details of the siting, design and external appearance of the building[s], the means of access thereto and the landscaping of the site (hereinafter called "the reserved matters") shall be obtained from the local planning authority in writing before any development is commenced (*paragraph 43*).

Appropriate in its entirety only where the outline application contained details of none of the items described as "reserved matters" in Article 1(2) of the Town and Country Planning (General Development Procedure) Order 1995.

3. Plans and particulars of the reserved matters referred to in condition 2 above, relating to the siting, design and external appearance of any buildings to be erected, the means of access to the site and the landscaping of the site, shall be submitted in writing to the local planning authority and shall be carried out as approved (*paragraph 43*).

4. Application for approval of the reserved matters shall be made to the local planning authority before the expiration of [three] years from the date of this permission (*paragraph 55*).

5. The development hereby permitted shall be begun either before the expiration of [five] years from the date of this permission, or before the expiration of [two] years from the date of approval of the last of the reserved matters to be approved, whichever is the later (*paragraph 55*).

Noise

6. .... [*activities*] shall not take place anywhere on the site except within building[s].

The condition should describe precisely the activities to be controlled as well as the particular building(s) in which they are to take place.

7.   The building shall be [constructed/adapted] so as to provide sound insulation against internally generated noise of not less than .... dB(A)[8], with windows shut and other means of ventilation provided.

Other methods of specifying sound insulation are given in BS 5821, Part 3: 1984, but this is likely to be replaced by a European Standard.

8.   The level of noise emitted from the site shall not exceed [A] dB between [T] and [T] Monday to Friday and [A] dB at any other time, as measured on the [specified boundary/boundaries] of the site at [location(s) of monitoring point(s)].

Specify: A—noise level expressed as LAeq, T over a time period X (e.g. 1 hour)
      T—time of day

9.   No [specified machinery] shall be operated on the premises before [time in the morning] on weekdays and [time in the morning] on Saturdays nor after [time in the evening] on weekdays and [time in the evening] on Saturdays, nor at any time on Sundays or Bank Holidays.

10. Before [any] [specified plant and/or machinery] is used on the premises, it shall be [enclosed with sound-insulating material] [and] [mounted in a way which will minimise transmission of structure borne sound] in accordance with a scheme to be approved in writing by the local planning authority.

Advice should be appended to the permission indicating the sound insulation required, or the maximum permitted noise level at a specified monitoring point.

11. Construction work shall not begin until a scheme for protecting the proposed [noise-sensitive development] from noise from the .... has been submitted and approved by the local planning authority; all works which form part of the scheme shall be completed before [any part of] the [noise-sensitive development(s)] is occupied.

Authorities should give applicants guidance on the maximum noise levels to be permitted within or around the noise-sensitive development so as to provide precise guidelines for the scheme to be permitted.

Aerodromes

12. The total number of aircraft movements shall not exceed [ ] per [period of time] except in an emergency.

13. Aircraft movements shall take place only between [hours of day] on [days of week], except in an emergency.

---

[8]PPG24: Planning and Noise (England only), gives advice on the use of planning powers to minimise the impact of noise. Explanations of the technical terms used above are contained in the glossary to PPG24.

Further model conditions which control noise by restricting use of an aerodrome or part of an aerodrome are contained in Annex 4 to PPG24: Planning and Noise (England only).

Accesses

14.   Means of vehicular access to the permitted building shall be from .... Road only.

15.   The building shall not be occupied until a means of vehicular access has been constructed in accordance with the approved plans.

16.   The building shall not be occupied until a means of access for [pedestrians and/or cyclists] has been constructed in accordance with the approved plans.

17.   Development shall not begin until details of the junction between the proposed service road and the highway have been approved in writing by the local planning authority; and the building shall not be occupied until that junction has been constructed in accordance with the approved details.

18.   No structure or erection exceeding .... metres in height shall be placed to the [east] of a line from .... to .... [as shown on the plan attached hereto].

To preserve site lines at a junction.

Service roads

19.   No [dwelling] shall be occupied until that part of the service road which provides access to it has been constructed in accordance with the approved plans (*paragraph 69*).

Parking

20.   No [dwelling] shall be occupied until space has been laid out within the site [in accordance with the plan attached] for [*number*] cars to be parked [and for the loading and unloading of [*number*] vehicles] [and for vehicles to turn so that they may enter and leave the site in forward gear].

21.   No [dwelling] shall be occupied until space has been laid out within the site [in accordance with the plan attached] for [number] bicycles to be parked.

22.   The building shall not be occupied until the area shown .... on the plan attached hereto has been drained and surfaced [*or other steps as may be specified*] [in accordance with details submitted and approved by the local planning authority], and that area shall not thereafter be used for any purpose other than the parking of vehicles.

Transport

23.   Development shall not commence until details of the proposed [bus/ railway] station(s) or stop(s) have been approved in writing by the local

planning authority; and the building(s) shall not be occupied until [that/those] stations(s) or stop(s) have been constructed in accordance with the approved plans.

Play areas

24. The building shall not be occupied until the area shown .... on the plan attached hereto has been laid out in accordance with [*specify relevant plan or drawing*], and that area shall not thereafter be used for nay purpose other than as a play area.

Landscape design proposals[9]

25. No development shall take place until full details of both hard and soft landscape works have been submitted to and approved in writing by the local planning authority and these works shall be carried out as approved. These details shall include [proposed finished levels or contours; means of enclosure; car parking layouts; other vehicle and pedestrian access and circulation areas; hard surfacing materials; minor artefacts and structures (*e.g.* furniture, play equipment, refuse or other storage units, signs, lighting etc.); proposed and existing functional services above and below ground (*e.g.* drainage power, communications cables, pipelines etc. indicating lines, manholes, supports etc); retained historic landscape features and proposals for restoration, where relevant.]

26. Soft landscape works shall include [planting plans; written specifications (including cultivation and other operations associated with plant and grass establishment); schedules of plants, noting species, plant sizes and proposed numbers/densities where appropriate; implementation programme] (*paragraphs* 48-50).

Landscape works implementation

27. All hard and soft landscape works shall be carried out in accordance with the approved details. The works shall be carried out prior to the occupation of any part of the development or in accordance with the programme agreed with the local planning authority (*paragraphs 48-50*).

28. No development shall take place until details of earthworks have been submitted to and approved in writing by the local planning authority. These details shall include the proposed grading and mounding of land areas including the levels and contours to be formed, showing the relationship of proposed mounding to existing vegetation and surrounding landform. Development shall be carried out in accordance with the approved details.

29. Details of any floodlighting shall be submitted to and approved in writing by the local planning authority before [the use hereby permitted commences]

[9]Model conditions 28-30 are based on conditions contained in "Model Landscape Planning Conditions" produced by Hampshire Local Government Landscape Group.

[and] [the building(s) is/are occupied]. Development shall be carried out in accordance with the approved details.

30. No development shall take place until there has been submitted to and approved in writing by the local planning authority a plan indicating the positions, design, materials and type of boundary treatment to be erected. The boundary treatment shall be completed before [the use hereby permitted is commenced] or [before the building(s) is/are occupied] or [in accordance with a timetable agreed in writing with the local planning authority]. Development shall be carried out in accordance with the approved details.

Landscape management plan
31. A landscape management plan, including long term design objectives, management responsibilities and maintenance schedules for all landscape areas, other than small, privately owned, domestic gardens, shall be submitted to and approved by the local planning authority prior to the occupation of the development or any phase of the development, whichever is the sooner, for its permitted use. The landscape management plan shall be carried out as approved.

32. No development shall take place until a schedule of landscape maintenance for a minimum period of [ ] years has been submitted to and approved in writing by the local planning authority. The schedule shall include details of the arrangements for its implementation. Development shall be carried out in accordance with the approved schedule (*paragraph 50*).

Storage
33. [Scrap] material shall not be stacked or deposited to a height exceeding .... metres.

Where open air storage is permitted.

34. No [timber] [propane or butane gas] shall be stored with .... metres of the [specified] boundary of the site.

Where necessary to avoid a fire hazard.

Personal permissions
35. The use hereby permitted shall be carried on only by [name of person] and shall be for a limited period being the period (of .... years from the date of this letter, or the period) during which the premises are occupied by [name of person] whichever is the shorter (*paragraph 93*).

36. When the premises case to be occupied by [name of person] or at the end (of .... years) whichever shall first occur, the use hereby permitted shall cease [and all materials and equipment brought on to the premises in connection with the use shall be removed].

Access for disabled people

37. Before the development hereby permitted is commenced a scheme indicating the provision to be made for disabled people to gain access to [ ] shall have been submitted to and approved by the local planning authority. The agreed scheme shall be implemented before the development hereby permitted is brought into use (*paragraph 114*).

Drainage

38. None of the dwellings shall be occupied until the [sewage disposal] [drainage] works have been completed in accordance with the submitted plans.

39. None of the dwellings shall be occupied until works for the disposal of sewage have been provided on the site to serve the development hereby permitted, in accordance with details to be submitted to and approved in writing by the local planning authority.

It may be necessary for the local planning authority to consult the water authority about the sewage disposal arrangements but this should not form part of any condition.

40. Development shall not begin until drainage works have been carried out in accordance with details to be submitted to and approved in writing by the local planning authority.

Temporary permission: reinstatement

41. [The building hereby permitted shall be removed] [The use hereby permitted shall be discontinued] and the land restored to its former condition on or before .... [*date*] in accordance with a scheme of work submitted to and approved by the local planning authority (*paragraph 113*).

An agreed note showing the condition of the site before works begin should be attached to a permission granted subject to this condition.

Staging of development

42. The works comprised in [*specified part*] of the development hereby permitted shall not be commenced before the works comprised in [*specified part*] are completed.

Where a proposal involves a number of separate parts, e.g. 100 houses on site a, 10 shops and a car park on site B, and 100 houses on site C, it may be desirable to prescribe by condition the order in which—but not the time when—the parts shall be carried out (paragraph 63).

Caravans: seasonal sites

43. [No caravan on the site shall be occupied] [No caravan shall remain on the site] between [date] in any one year and [date] in the succeeding year (*paragraph 115*).

Commercial of industrial building: limitation on occupancy

44. Until .... [*normally not more than 10 years ahead*] the premises shall be occupied only by a person, firm, company or other organisation which was, immediately prior to occupying the accommodation to which this permission relates, in occupation for at least [two] years of premises within the County of .... used as a [general or light industrial building] [warehouse] [office] (*paragraphs 94-95*).

This condition needs to be supported by restraint policies in the development plan.

Agricultural workers' condition

45. The occupation of the dwelling shall be limited to a person solely or mainly working, or last working, in the locality in agriculture or in forestry, or a widow or widower of such a person, and to any resident dependants (*paragraphs 102-105*).

Staff accommodation

46. The occupation of the dwelling shall be limited to a person solely or mainly employed or last employed in the business occupying the plot edged red on the attached plan, or a widow or widower of such a person, or any resident dependants (*paragraphs 100-101*).

"Granny" annexes

47. The extension (building) hereby permitted shall not be occupied at any time other than for purposes ancillary to the residential use of the dwelling know as [ ] (*paragraphs 98-99*).

Restriction on use

48. The premises shall be used for .... and for no other purpose (including any other purpose in Class .... of the Schedule to the Town and Country Planning (Use Classes) Order 1987, or in any provision equivalent to that Class in any statutory instrument revoking and re-enacting that Order with or without modification) (*paragraph 90*).

49. The premises shall not be used for the sale of food for consumption off the premises other than confectionery (*paragraph 90*).

To prevent e.g. a retail DIY warehouse from being used as a food supermarket.

Restrictions on permitted development

50. Notwithstanding the provisions of the Town and Country Planning (General Permitted Development) Order 1995 (or any order revoking and re-enacting that Order with or without modification), no garages shall be erected [other than those expressly authorised by this permission] (*paragraphs 86-88*).

51. Notwithstanding the provisions of the Town and Country Planning (General Permitted Development) Order 1995 (or any order revoking and re-enacting that Order with or without modification), no fences, gates or walls shall be erected within the curtilage of any dwellinghouse forward of any wall of that dwellinghouse which fronts onto a road (*paragraphs 86-88*).

Where there is sufficient merit in an open plan housing layout to justify control of front fencing.

52. Notwithstanding the provisions of the Town and Country Planning (General Permitted Development) Order 1995 (or any order revoking and re-enacting that Order with or without modification), no windows/dormer windows [other than those expressly authorised by this permission] shall be constructed.

Sites of archaeological interest (not scheduled or designated under 1979 Act)

53. No development shall take place until fencing has been erected, in a manner to be agreed with the local planning authority, about [*insert name of monument*]; and no works shall take place within the area inside that fencing without the consent of the local planning authority (*paragraphs 80-81*).

54. The developer shall afford access at all reasonable times to any archaeologist nominated by the local planning authority, and shall allow him to observe the excavations and record items of interest and finds (*paragraphs 80-81*).

Conditions should not require work to be held up while archaeological investigation takes place, though some developers may be willing to give such facilities.

55. No development shall take place within the area indicated (this would be the area of archaeological interest) until the applicant, or their agents or successors in title, has secured the implementation of a programme of archaeological work in accordance with a written scheme of investigation which has been submitted by the applicant and approved in writing by the local planning authority.

Developers will wish to ensure that in drawing up a scheme, the timetable for the investigation is included within the details of the agreed scheme.

Contaminated land

56. Development shall not begin until a scheme to deal with contamination of the site has been submitted to and approved in writing by the local planning authority.

57. The above scheme shall include an investigation and assessment to identify the extent of contamination and the measures to be taken to avoid risk to the [public/buildings/environment] when the site is developed.

58. Development shall not commence until the measures approved in the scheme have been implemented.

Where investigation/remedial proposals carried out/agreed before planning permission granted.

Soil decontamination[10]
59. Before the development hereby permitted commences on the site, a soil survey of the site shall be undertaken and the results provided to the local planning authority. The survey shall be taken at such points and to such depth as the local planning authority may stipulate. A scheme for decontamination of the site shall be submitted to and approved by the local planning authority in writing and the scheme as approved shall be fully implemented and completed before any [residential] unit hereby permitted is first occupied.

For use where soil contamination is known or suspected.

Density
60. The development hereby permitted shall not exceed a density of [ ] habitable rooms per hectare.

Height of building
61. No building on any part of the development hereby permitted shall exceed [ ] storeys in height.

Balconies
62. The roof area of the extension hereby permitted shall not be used as a balcony, roof garden or similar amenity area without the grant of further specific permission from the local planning authority.

Matching materials
63. The materials to be used in the construction of the external surfaces of the extension hereby permitted shall match those used in the existing building.

64. No development shall take place until samples of the materials to be used in the construction of the external surfaces of the extension hereby permitted have been submitted to and approved in writing by the local planning authority. Development shall be carried out in accordance with the approved details.

Hours of use (industrial)
65. No machinery shall be operated, no process shall be carried out and no deliveries taken at or despatched from the site outside the following time [ ] nor at any time on Sundays, Bank or Public Holidays.

[10]Model conditions 59-63, 65-70, and 76-78 are reproduced with the permission of Sweet and Maxwell Limited and are contained in *Planning Law Practice and Precedents* – Editors Stephen Tromans and Robert Turrall-Clarke.

Hours of use (restaurants etc)

66. The use hereby permitted shall not be open to customers outside the follow times [ ].

67. No amplified or other music shall be played in the premises outside the following time [ ].

Hours of deliveries

68. No deliveries shall be taken at or despatched from the site outside the hours of [ ] nor at any time on Sundays, Bank or Public Holidays.

Petrol filling stations

69. The site shall only be used as a petrol filling station, and no part shall be used for the sale display, or repair of vehicles.

70. The premises shall not be open for business, nor shall supplies of fuel be delivered thereto, outside the hours of [ ].

Trees

Outline permissions

Location of trees on and adjacent to development sites

71. The plans and particulars submitted in accordance with condition [ ] above shall include:

    (a) a plan showing the location of, and allocating a reference number to, each existing tree on the site which has a stem with a diameter, measured over the bark at a point 1.5 metres above ground level, exceeding 75 mm, showing which trees are to be retained and the crown spread of each retained tree;

    (b) details of the species, diameter (measured in accordance with paragraph (a) above), and the approximate height, and an assessment of the general state of health and stability, of each retained tree and of each tree which is on land adjacent to the site and to which paragraphs (c) and (d) below apply;

    (c) details of any proposed topping or lopping of any retained tree, or of any tree on land adjacent to the site;

    (d) details of any proposed alterations in existing ground levels, and of the position of any proposed excavation, [within the crown spread of any retained tree or of any tree on land adjacent to the site] [within a distance from any retained tree, or any tree on land adjacent to the site, equivalent to half the height of that tree];

    (e) details of the specification and position of fencing [and of any other measures to be taken] for the protection of any retained tree from damage before or during the course of development.

In this condition "retained tree" means an existing tree which is to be retained in accordance with the plan referred to in paragraph (a) above.

72.   The plans and particulars submitted in accordance with condition [ ] above shall include details of the size, species, and positions or density of all trees to be planted, and the proposed time of planting.

Detailed planning permissions

Provision for tree planting

73.   No works or development shall take place until full details of all proposed tree planting, and the proposed times of planting, have been approved in writing by the local planning authority, and all tree planting shall be carried out in accordance with those details and at those times.

74.   If within a period of [two years] from the date of the planting of any tree that tree, or any tree planted in replacement for it, is removed, uprooted or destroyed or dies, [or becomes, in the opinion of the local planning authority, seriously damaged or defective,] another tree of the same species and size as that originally planted shall be planted at the same place, unless the local planning authority gives its written consent to any variation.

Existing trees which are to be retained

75.   In this condition "retained tree" means an existing tree which is to be retained in accordance with the approved plans and particulars; and paragraphs (a) and (b) below shall have effect until the expiration of [1 year[11]] from [the date of the occupation of the building for its permitted use].

(a) No retained tree shall be cut down, uprooted or destroyed, nor shall any retained tree be topped or lopped other than in accordance with the approved plans and particulars, without the written approval of the local planning authority. Any topping or lopping approved shall be carried out in accordance with British Standard [3998 (Tree Work)].

(b) If any retained tree is removed, uprooted or destroyed or dies, another tree shall be planted at the same place and that tree shall be of such size and species, and shall be planted at such time, as may be specified in writing by the local planning authority.

(c) The erection of fencing for the protection of any retained tree shall be undertaken in accordance with the approved plans and particulars before any equipment, machinery or materials are brought on to the site for the purposes of the development, and shall be maintained until all equipment, machinery and surplus materials have been removed from the site. Nothing shall be stored or placed in any area fenced in

---

[11]A specific time limit should be included. It is not considered to be reasonable to use conditions as an alternative to tree preservation orders to secure long-term protection of trees.

accordance with this condition and the ground levels within those areas shall not be altered, nor shall any excavation be made, without the written consent of the local planning authority.

Amenity land

Provision of amenity land
76. None of the building operations hereby permitted shall be carried out on that part of the application site shown .... on the submitted/attached plan.

77. The details of the landscaping of the site required to be submitted shall include details of a scheme for the preservation or laying out of that part of the application site shown .... on the submitted/attached plan as amenity land.

Laying out of land allocated as amenity land
78. Before/within 12 months from the date when the change of use hereby permitted is carried out/any of the buildings permitted are occupied/any of the buildings permitted are first used for the purpose of [   ] the land shown on the permitted plan as [   ] shall be laid out in accordance with that plan as amenity land.

Prior approval
79. With respect to any condition that requires the prior written approval of the local planning authority, the works thereby approved shall be carried out in accordance with that approval unless subsequently otherwise approved in writing by that local planning authority.

Appendix B

Conditions which are unacceptable

Conditions of the following kinds are NOT acceptable (guidance on the reasons for this is given in the Annex above; references to the relevant paragraphs of the annex are given in these examples):

1. To require that a development shall be *completed* within a time limit (*paragraph 61 of the Annex above*).

2. To require that means of access shall be set back and splayed in agreement with the local highway authority, when the latter are a third party (*paragraph 38*).

3.   To require that no advertisements shall be displayed on the site. It is preferable for control of outdoor advertising to be exercised by means of the relevant provision in the Town and Country Planning (Control of Advertisements) Regulations 1992. Planning conditions should not normally be used to control advertisements (*paragraph 21*).

4.   To require that the land in front of the buildings shall be made available for future road widening. This condition improperly requires land to be made available as part of the highway (*paragraph 72*).

5.   To require that a lay-by shall be constructed and thereafter assigned to the highway authority (*paragraph 72*).

6.   To require that flats, for example, should not be occupied by more than .... persons. This condition is unsatisfactory in enforcement terms since it would be difficult to monitor and require an intolerable degree of supervision (*paragraphs 26 and 27*).

7.   To require that loading and unloading, and the parking of vehicles, shall not take place on the highway at the front of the premises. This condition purports to exercise control in respect of a public highway, which is not under the control of the applicant (*paragraph 37*).

8.   To require that the site shall be kept tidy at all times. This is vague and likely to be incapable of enforcement (*paragraph 31*).

9.   To require that the applicants shall construct an ancillary road as and when required by the local planning authority (*paragraph 30*).

10.   To require that the developer shall comply with the bylaws and general statutory provisions in force in the district. This condition is unrelated to planning control (*paragraph 20*).

11.   To require that furnishings *e.g.* the curtaining of a stage, shall be of a fireproof material. Fireproofing of furnishings of buildings is not a planning matter (*paragraph 22*).

12.   To require that aircraft should only arrive or depart at an aerodrome on specified air traffic routes. This condition deals with an activity which is regulated by quite different statutory provisions and may well be unenforceable if the aerodrome developer is not responsible for air traffic control *i.e.* where air traffic routeing is the responsibility of the Civil Aviation Authority or the National Air Traffic Service (*paragraphs 22 and 37*).

13.   To require that a shop window display be maintained in an attractive condition. Such a condition provides no certain and objective criterion by which it could be enforced (*paragraph 31*).

APPENDIX 2

Circular No 16/91: Planning and Compensation Act 1991 Planning Obligations[1]

1.   Annex A to this Circular describes certain of the provisions in sections 12 and 83 of the Planning and Compensation Act 1991 which will be brought into effect by commencement order on October 25. The provisions are: that part of section 12(1) which substitutes a new section 106 for section 106 of the Town and Country Planning Act 1990; section 12(2) and (3); and section 83.

2.   The Department intends to bring into force the remainder of section 12(1) (*i.e.* new sections 106A and 106B of the 1990 Act) by commencement order in Spring 1992, accompanied by Regulations made under sections 106A and 106B and an explanatory Circular.

3.   Annex B to this Circular provides policy guidance to local planning authorities on the use to be made of planning obligations under new section 106 of the 1990 Act.

4.   Enquiries about this Circular may be addressed to PDC3 Division, Department of the Environment, Room C13/13, 2 Marsham Street, London SW1P 3EB (Tel: 071-276 3903) or the Planning Division, Welsh Office, Cathays Park, Cardiff CR1 3NQ (Tel: 0222 823869).

Annex A

Planning and Compensation Act 1991
Planning obligations and consequential amendments

Planning obligations
A1.   *Section 12(1)* of the 1991 Act substitutes new sections 106, 106A and 106B for section 106 of the Town and Country Planning Act 1990. (New sections 106A

[1]Issued 8 October 1991 by the Department of the Environment and the Welsh Office (Circular 53/91).

and 106B are not dealt with in this Annex.) New section 106 introduces the concept of planning obligations, which comprises both planning agreements and unilateral undertakings. It enables a planning obligation to be entered into by means of a unilateral undertaking by a developer as well as by agreement between a developer and a local planning authority.

A2. *New section 106(1)* provides that anyone with an interest in land may enter into a planning obligation enforceable by the local planning authority identified in the instrument creating the obligation. Such an obligation may be created by agreement or by the person with the interest making an undertaking. The use of the new term "planning obligation" reflects the fact that obligations may now be created other than by agreement between the parties (that is, by the developer making an undertaking). Such obligations may restrict development or use of the land; require operations or activities to be carried out in, on, under or over the land; require the land to be used in any specified way; or require payments to be made to the authority either in a single sum or periodically.

A3. The obligations created run with the land (as do planning agreements made under old section 106 of the 1990 Act) so they may be enforced against both the original covenantor and against anyone acquiring an interest in the land from him. The obligations can be positive (requiring the covenantor or his successors in title to do a specified thing in, on, under or over the land) or negative (restricting the covenantor or his successors from developing or using the land in a specified way). Planning agreements have commonly been made both under section 106 and under section 33 of the Local Government (Miscellaneous Provisions) Act 1982 which provides expressly for positive covenants. It will no longer be necessary for section 33 of the 1982 Act to be used in the planning context, given the scope of new section 106. The scope of section 33 has been confined to non-planning contexts by paragraph 6 of Schedule 7 to the 1991 Act.

A4. *New section 106(2)* provides that a planning obligation may:

 (i) be unconditional or subject to conditions;
 (ii) impose any restriction or requirement in 106(1)(a) to (c) for an indefinite or specified period (thus enabling, for instance, an obligation to end when a planning permission expires);
 (iii) provide for payments of money to be made, either of a specific amount or by reference to a formula, and require periodical payments to be paid indefinitely or for a specified period.

A5. *New section 106(3)* provides that, as at present with agreements, planning obligations shall be enforceable against the original covenantor and his successors in title.

A6. *New section 106(4)* enables the instrument which creates the planning obligations to limit the liability of covenantors to the period before they cease to have an interest in the land. This enables someone entering into a planning obligation to cease to be bound by its terms once he has disposed of his interest in the land concerned.

A7. *New sections 106(5), (6), (7) and (8)* contain new provisions for enforcing planning obligations. *New section 106(5)* provides for restrictions or requirements imposed under a planning obligation to be enforced by injunction. *New section 106(6)* provides that, in addition to 106(5), if the developer is in breach of a requirement to carry out works on the land, the authority may enter the land and do so itself and recover its reasonable expenses. *New section 106(7)* provides that the authority, before exercising its powers to enter the land, shall give not less than 21 days' notice of its intention to do so to any person against whom the obligation is enforceable. *New section 106(8)* provides that any person who wilfully obstructs the authority if it enters the land under subsection (6)(a) shall be guilty of an offence and be liable to a fine of up to level 3 on the standard scale (currently £400).

A8. *New section 106(9)* requires for the first time that a planning obligation may only be entered into by a deed which: states that the obligation created is a planning obligation; identifies the land concerned; identifies the person entering into the obligation and states his interest; and identifies the authority by whom the obligation may be enforced. *New section 106(10)* requires a copy of the deed to be given to the local planning authority by whom it is enforceable.

A9. *New section 106(11)* provides that a planning obligation is a local land charge for the purposes of the Local Land Charges Act 1975. If a local land charge is not registered, it remains binding against a purchaser of the land, but the purchaser is entitled to compensation for non-registration. Under section 8 of the 1975 Act any member of the public has a right of access to the local land charges register, which is maintained by every London borough and district council. The register contains a description of the charge, including a reference to the relevant statutory provision, and says where relevant documents may be inspected.

A10. *New section 106(12)* enables the Secretary of State to make regulations specifying that money to be paid or expenses recoverable under a planning obligation shall be a charge on the land. This would assist a local planning authority in proceedings to recover such sums. (The Department has no immediate plans to make regulations under this subsection.)

A11. *New section 106(13)* defines the terms "land" and "specified" used in new section 106.

A12. *Section 12(2)* makes an insertion into section 296(2) of the 1990 Act so that the local planning authority may not enforce a planning obligation against Crown land, either by injunction or by entering the land, without the consent of the "appropriate authority" (*i.e.* the Crown body responsible for the land concerned).

A13. *Section 12(3)* inserts a new section 299A into the 1990 Act. *New section 299A(1)* provides that the appropriate authority may enter into a planning obligation in relation to any Crown or Duchy interest in land. The obligation is enforceable to the extent mentioned in new section 299A(3). *New section 299A(2)* provides that a planning obligation under new section 299A may only be entered by an instrument executed as a deed which: states that the obligation concerned is a planning obligation; identifies the land concerned; identifies the appropriate authority and states the Crown or Duchy interest; and identifies the local planning authority by whom the obligation may be enforced. *New section 299A(3)* provides that a planning obligation under this section may be enforced against any person with a private interest derived from a Crown or Duchy interest. *New section 299A(4)* applies most of the provisions of new sections 106, 106A and 106B to obligations entered into under new section 299A. *New section 299A(5)* requires the consent of the appropriate authority to be obtained before a planning obligation in respect of Crown or Duchy land is enforced.

Consequential amendments
A14. *Section 83* of the 1991 Act, which applies to England and Wales, Scotland and Northern Ireland, amends section 91A of the Income and Corporation Taxes Act 1988, consequential upon section 12. Section 91A of the 1988 Act provides that, where a person makes a site restoration payment in the course of carrying on a trade, the payment shall be allowable as a deduction against profits or gains for the relevant tax period.

Annex B

Planning obligations

B1. This guidance gives advice on the proper use of planning obligations made under section 106 of the Town and Country Planning Act 1990 (as substituted by section 12 of the Planning and Compensation Act 1991) and of similar obligations under other powers including local legislation. The guidance substantially re-affirms, with some amendment, the advice given in Department of the Environment Circular 22/83 (Welsh Office Circular 46/83), which it supersedes.

Definition
B2. The term "planning gain" has no statutory significance and is not found in the Planning Acts. The whole planning process is intended to operate in the public interest, in that it is chiefly aimed at securing economy, efficiency and amenity in the development and use of land. This is achieved through the normal

process of development plan preparation and the exercise of development control. In granting planning permission, or in negotiations with developers and other interests that lead to the grant of planning permission, the local planning authority may seek to secure modifications or improvements to the proposals submitted for their approval. They may grant permission subject to conditions, and where appropriate they may seek to enter into planning obligations with a developer regarding the use or development of the land concerned or of other land or buildings. Rightly used, planning obligations may enhance development proposals.

B3.   By these means the local planning authority can aim to ensure that new development or redevelopment is facilitated while having regard to the interest of the local environment and other planning considerations. The term "planning gain" has come to be used very loosely to apply both to this normal and legitimate operation of the planning system and also to attempts to extract from developers payments in cash or in kind for purposes that are not directly related to the development proposed but are sought as "the price of planning permission". Equally, the term "planning gain" has been used to describe offers from developers to a local authority that are not related to their development proposal. The Planning Acts do not envisage that planning powers should be used for such purposes, and in this sense "planning gain" is outside the scope of the planning process. Since the term "planning gain" is imprecise and misleading, it is not used in this policy guidance, which relates to the role of planning obligations in the proper exercise of development control.

B4.   This guidance is not concerned directly with matters arising from other legislation, *e.g.* the requisitioning of the provision of a water supply or of a public sewer from a water company under the Water Act 1989 or previous legislation; or agreements made under the Public Health Act 1936; or agreements about development in the vicinity of trunk roads under section 278 of the Highways Act 1980 (as substituted by the New Roads and Street Works Act 1991), on which the Department of Transport and the Welsh Office are considering revised advice to supersede Circular Roads 1/89 (Welsh Office 13/89). Insofar as such arrangements are made in connection with the grant of planning permission however, this guidance is relevant in those circumstances.

General policy
B5.   The following paragraphs set out the circumstances in which certain types of benefit can reasonably be sought in connection with a grant of planning permission. They are the circumstances to which the Secretary of State and his inspectors will have regard in determining applications or appeals. They may be briefly stated as those circumstances where the benefit sought is related to the development and necessary to the grant of permission. Local planning authorities should ensure that the presence or absence of extraneous inducements or benefits does not influence their decision on the planning

application. Authorities should bear in mind that their decision may be challenged in the courts if it is suspected of having been improperly influenced.

B6. Planning applications should be considered on their merits and determined in accordance with the provisions of the development plan unless material considerations indicate otherwise. It may be reasonable, depending on the circumstances, either to impose conditions on the grant of planning permission, or (where the planning objection to a development proposal cannot be overcome by means of a condition) to seek to enter a planning obligation by agreement with the applicant which would be associated with any permission granted. If there is a choice between imposing conditions and entering into a planning obligation, the imposition of a condition is preferable because it enables a developer to appeal to the Secretary of State. The terms of conditions imposed on a planning permission should not be re-stated in a planning obligation, because that would entail nugatory duplication and frustrate a developer's right of appeal.

B7. As with conditions (see DOE Circular 1/85, Welsh Office Circular 1/85), planning obligations should only be sought where they are necessary to the granting of permission, relevant to planning, and relevant to the development to be permitted. Unacceptable development should never be permitted because of unrelated benefits offered by the applicant, nor should an acceptable development be refused permission simply because the applicant is unable or unwilling to offer such unrelated benefits.

B8. The test of the reasonableness of seeking a planning obligation from an applicant for planning permission depends on whether what is required:

(1) is needed to enable the development to go ahead, for example the provision of adequate access or car parking; or

(2) in the case of financial payment will contribute to meeting the cost of providing such facilities in the near future; or

(3) is otherwise so directly related to the proposed development and to the use of the land after its completion, that the development ought not to be permitted without it, *e.g.* the provision, whether by the applicant or by the authority at the applicant's expense, of car parking in or near the development, or reasonable amounts of open space related to the development, or of social, educational, recreational, sporting or other community provision the need for which arises from the development; or

(4) is designed in the case of mixed development to secure an acceptable balance of uses; or to secure the implementation of local plan policies for a particular area or type of development (*e.g.* the inclusion of an element of affordable housing in a larger residential development); or

(5) is intended to offset the loss of or impact on any amenity or resource present on the site prior to development, for example in the interests of nature conservation. The Department welcomes the initiatives taken

by some developers in creating nature reserves, planting trees, establishing wildlife ponds and providing other nature conservation benefits. This echoes the Government's view in *This Common Inheritance* (Cm. 1200) that local authorities and developers should work together in the interest of preserving the natural environment.

Planning obligations can therefore relate to land, roads or buildings other than those covered by the planning permission, provided that there is a direct relationship between the two. But they should not be sought where this connection does not exist or is too remote to be considered reasonable.

B9. If what is required passes one of the tests set out in the preceding paragraph, a further test has to be applied. This is whether the extent of what is required is fairly and reasonably related in scale and kind to the proposed development. Thus a developer may reasonably be expected to pay for or contribute to the cost of infrastructure which would not have been necessary but for his development, but his payments should be directly related in scale to the benefit which the proposed development will derive from the facilities to be provided. So, for example, a developer may reach agreement with an infrastructure undertaker to bring forward in time a project which is already programmed but is some years from implementation.

B10. The costs of subsequent maintenance and other recurrent expenditure should normally be borne by the authority or body in which the asset is to be vested, and the planning authority should not attempt to impose commuted maintenance sums when considering the planning aspects of the development. Exceptions may be made, for example, where additional highway works are an essential pre-requisite to the granting of planning permission and an agreement is made under section 278 of the Highways Act 1980 (which specifically provides for maintenance payments) or in the case of small areas of open space or landscaping principally of benefit to the development itself rather than to the wider public.

Unilateral undertakings

B11. Section 106(1) of the Town and Country Planning Act 1990, as substituted by section 12 of the Planning and Compensation Act 1991, enables a developer to enter into a planning obligation by making a unilateral undertaking as an alternative to doing so by agreement. Undertakings are not intended to replace the use of agreements. It is reasonable for local planning authorities to expect developers to endeavour to resolve any planning objections the authority may have to the development proposal by agreement, but, equally, the authority should do its best to reach agreement and to seek to negotiate in accordance with this guidance. Where a developer considers that negotiations are being unnecessarily protracted or that unreasonable demands are being made, he may enter into a planning obligation by making a unilateral undertaking. A unilateral undertaking may be couched in conditional terms, promising to do or not to do certain things if, for example, planning permission is granted. A developer will then be bound once permission is granted, and the authority will be able to enforce the obligation against him.

B12. The use of unilateral undertakings is expected to be principally at appeal, where there are planning objections which only a planning obligation can resolve, but the parties cannot reach agreement. Where a developer offers an undertaking at appeal, it will be referred to the local planning authority to seek their views. such an undertaking should be in accordance with the general policy in this guidance. It should be relevant to planning and should resolve the planning objections to the development proposal concerned. Otherwise, it would not be a material consideration and will not be taken into account. If the undertaking would resolve an identified planning objection to a development proposal but also contains unrelated benefits, it should only be taken into account to the extent that it resolves the objections. Developers should not promise to do what they cannot perform. Attention is drawn to the statutory requirement that a developer must have an interest in the land before he can enter into a planning obligation. At appeal the Inspector may seek evidence of title if it has not been demonstrated that the developer has the requisite interest. Where a trunk road is involved the developer will also need the agreement of the relevant highway authorities and any necessary highway orders.

Public involvement

B13. Where planning obligations are to be sought regularly in connection with certain types of development the local planning authority's policy on this should be made clear in the local plan or in Part II of the unitary development plan, and should be justified by reference to the tests outlined in paragraphs B8-B9 above. More detailed advice on infrastructure and the preparation of development plans will be provided in PPG12 when it is updated within the next few months. The existence of policies should not preclude the negotiation of agreements on an *ad hoc* basis.

B14. Authorities are reminded that planning obligations must be registered on the local land charges register. Members of the public should be given every assistance in locating planning obligations which are of interest to them. Planning obligations and related correspondence should be listed as background papers to the committee report relating to the development proposal concerned (see section 100D of the Local Government Act 1972). Authorities would need a very strong case either to exclude the press and public when discussing a planning obligation or to determine that connected correspondence should be kept from public view. Authorities should not that section 100I of the 1972 Act confers order-making powers on the Secretary of State, which enable the categories of exemption from the access to information provisions to be changed.

Mineral workings

B15. Special considerations apply to the use of planning obligations and to the imposition of conditions in connection with mineral developments. These are set out in MPG2 (paragraphs 69 and 75), MPG7 (paragraphs 34 and 90) and DOE Circular 25/85 (WO 60/85).

Miscellaneous

B16. In the interests of speed, and if both parties agree, the first draft of an agreement creating a planning obligation may be prepared by the developer's solicitor or by a solicitor approved by the local planning authority whose fees are met by the developer.

B17. Local planning authorities are reminded that they should not use a planning obligation as a vehicle to require developers to follow policies or practices that would be unlawful for the authorities themselves.

B18. Under the new system of local authority capital finance established by Part IV of the Local Government and Housing Act 1989, if a planning obligation genuinely relates only to planning matters and there is no disposal of a capital asset by the local authority, then the goods or services received under the obligation are not capital receipts for the purposes of Part IC and the debt redemption provisions of the Act do not apply. Debt redemption will generally apply, however, if the planning obligation relates to the disposal of a capital asset or to any payment or repayment referred to in section 58(1) of the Act.

Conclusion

B19. This advice is intended to provide guidance to local authorities about the proper exercise of their statutory development control powers. The Secretary of State will deal with each planning application or appeal which comes before him on its merits but he is unlikely to support demands by local authorities which go beyond this guidance. If a planning authority seeks to impose unreasonable obligations in connection with a grant of planning permission it is open to the applicant to refuse to accept them; he has the right of appeal to the Secretary of State against a refusal of permission, or the imposition of a condition, or the non-determination of the application. Such appeals will be considered in the light of the advice given above. Where an appeal has arisen because of what seems to the Secretary of State to be an unreasonable demand on the part of the local planning authority, and a public local inquiry has been held, he will consider sympathetically any application which may be made to him for an award of costs.

Cancellation

B20. DOE Circular 22/83 (WO Circular 46/83) is cancelled.

Index